GOOD TOGETHER

Drink + feast
with Mr Lyan and friends

GOOD TOGETHER

Words and illustrations by Ryan Chetiyawardana

photographs by Kim Lightbody

FRANCES
LINCOLN

Good Together
© 2017 Quarto Publishing plc.
Text © Ryan Chetiyawardana 2017
Photographs © Kim Lightbody 2017
Commissioning editor: Zena Alkayat

First Published in 2017 by Frances Lincoln
An imprint of The Quarto Group
The Old Brewery, 6 Blundell Street,
London N7 9BH, United Kingdom
www.QuartoKnows.com

A catalogue record for this book is available from
the British Library.

ISBN 978-0-7112-3897-8

Printed and bound in China

1 2 3 4 5 6 7 8 9

Brimming with creative inspiration, how-to projects and useful
information to enrich your everyday life, Quarto Knows is a favourite
destination for those pursuing their interests and passions. Visit our
site and dig deeper with our books into your area of interest: Quarto
Creates, Quarto Cooks, Quarto Homes, Quarto Lives, Quarto Drives,
Quarto Explores, Quarto Gifts, or Quarto Kids.

There are too many people to thank who've been responsible for, or have helped shape, what I do. So this book is for everyone who regularly helps me bring to life what I love. Food and drink might not save the world, but people committing themselves to what's right and what they love certainly will.

Anette, my dad and my brother have all saved me - figuratively and literally, at some point - but this book is for mum. Thank you, sorry, and I hope you know we wholeheartedly appreciate all the sacrifices and endless love. The little things were and are everything, and I'm eternally grateful.

CONTENTS

INTRODUCTION
RYAN CHETIYAWARDANA

When I ask a friend how they are, they'll inevitably reply: 'Busy.' I'm guilty of it too – it's a symptom of the modern world. But it only confirms the need for quality time spent with the people you love. The more you do it, the more you understand it's what really matters – good times with friends and family are the most effective panacea for a busy week/month/year. 'Quality' is the key word, though; excess can be great but it's rarely memorable! Given that bringing friends together is harder amid today's fast-paced lifestyles, making these moments properly memorable should be a priority. This book is about how good it is to bring people together, and how good food and drink brought together can help you have a better time with the people you love.

In my first book, 'Good Things to Drink', I talked about the worlds of food and drink being one and the same, and that they should be treated that way. And also how the right food and drink can help shape the mood of an occasion. It has been great to see so many dog-eared, stained and worn copies of the book in people's houses, where the recipes had been brought to life. I love getting tagged in Instagram photos showing people adapting recipes to their own tastes and using the drinks to fit their lives. I wanted to expand on that here, helping you bring your friends together using amazing food, as well as drink.

So for *Good Together*, I called on some of my favourite friends from the world of food, and some of the best chefs in the world. This isn't about trying to reproduce dishes from their (excellent!) restaurants. (I've not included drinks from my bars – no one wants to spend hours prepping a multitude of complicated steps; it's much smarter to have something that's still exciting and delicious, but straightforward to make.) The recipes are here to inspire, and the chefs offer brilliant advice and ideas.

It's important to note that this isn't a party planner (no parties are the same, and where would the fun be if this was a rulebook?), and it's also not about cocktail pairing. This is a guide to drinks and dishes that fit a particular mood or occasion – be it a cosy night in or a summer BBQ – and also work well together. It's all very adaptable, and easily ownable. For example, where I've suggested a gin, you can substitute vodka. Likewise, if you don't like any of the herbs and spices, adjust the recipes to your tastes. Experimentation, trial and error is all part of the fun (I also think you learn more, or at least faster, when things go belly up!).

I hope you find this book beautiful (thanks to my family and friends), interesting (it's a slightly voyeuristic look into the personal lives of some of the best people in the world of food and drink if nothing else!) and, most importantly, useful!

ABOUT THE CHEFS

So who are these lovely peeps, and why are they suggesting dishes for you to make for your loved ones? I'm very thankful to call many of them close friends, but they're all people who have made food (usually in their professional rather than personal environment) that's helped me have some of my most memorable times with others.

They are incredible chefs, often topping 'world best' lists, and I'd wholeheartedly recommend visiting their establishments. Their restaurants go beyond the edible offering – these chefs are at the top of the game in terms of creating harmony between food and setting. But the atmosphere and food they create at work is very different to how they eat, drink and entertain in their homes, so I asked them to suggest something that's personal and authentic to them, and reflects what they make when they want to get together with those close to them.

Good cooking is so much more than kitchen skills. It requires a sensitivity to who you're cooking for, the setting, when you're cooking it, and why. It could be midwinter and time for comfort food to indulge in with your partner; it could be a glorious summer's day where a few light bites, sherry-based drinks and a chatter with friends is in order. The right food and drink brought together can help create truly special times. The chef's professional insight means that each of their recipes is smattered with little gems of knowledge and (in some cases) some pretty unusual techniques. Hopefully the ideas and recipes (together with the cocktails) will inspire you to create your own special gatherings.

Richard Hart
Tartine Bakery
San Francisco
P021

The legendary bread at Tartine Bakery was something I'd heard about from my pal Todd Selby, who'd featured the San Francisco bakery in his 'Edible Selby' book. Lee from Black Axe Mangal (see opposite) had also spoken very highly of Richard Hart, the head baker there. All this created pretty high expectations for the carb-loaded fare that slides out of Tartine's ovens. And rest assured, you should absolutely believe the hype.

I'm a huge fan of proper bread (and real butter!). I even try to convince friends who avoid gluten to at least try real bread made with fresh flour (not the stuff that's been in your cupboard for weeks, and away from the field for frighteningly longer). To me the difference between real bread and supermarket loaves is chalk and cheese, and Richard's delicious stuffed bread recipe is a case in point. It's the perfect thing to break with friends.

Nieves Barragán Mohacho
Barrafina
London
P029

Many Londoners (and those from further afield) will put Barrafina at the top of their 'must visits' (and revisit!). Once you've tried Nieves's food, it's pretty easy to understand why. Along with a bottle of sherry (they have an ace En Rama if you do get the chance to go), the food instantly takes you to a sunnier place, regardless of the weather outside, and is instantly relaxing.

It was only fitting then to ask her to suggest what she cooks for having friends round for some outdoor bites. And what's magical is that her food brings to mind balmy alfresco days even if you don't have the luxury of a garden. I've created drinks that fit this mood too: ideal if you're outside, but bright enough to transport you there if you just want to escape a miserable afternoon.

Douglas McMaster
Silo
Brighton, UK
P037

Me and the Lyan team have been proponents of a more sustainable, considered style of hospitality since we started out. And being mindful of the waste we all generate was part of my family life growing up. White Lyan pioneered the idea of addressing the amount of waste that ended up in the bin or down the drain, and for many years friends had tried to introduce me to the very likeminded Doug. What really blew me away when we finally met was Doug's creativity. He practised 'zero waste' cookery in a more advanced form than anyone I knew, but regardless of this admirable task, he made sensationally exciting and delicious food.

The dishes he's created, and the drinks they've inspired me to make, take the idea of zero-waste far beyond its ethical purpose, towards something that makes your brain dance in a whole new way (seriously)!

James Lowe
Lyle's
London
P047

I met James when he was doing his first pop-up as part of the Young Turks (along with Isaac McHale – see p17 – and Ben Greeno). I was amazed by the quality of what these three young chefs were doing. There's a simplicity James achieves in his food that hides both the skill and the intellect behind it, and what's impressive is how he sources the right ingredients and lets them shine in the most wonderful way. No doubt some of this is because he was taught by Fergus Henderson during his time as head chef at St. John, but James very much has his own style.

For the recipes in this book, I'd suggest getting hold of a truly exceptional crop of ingredients, and follow James's lead. I've done that with the cocktails and focused on some star ingredients, including the best pears and rhubarb I could find.

Tom Oldroyd
Oldroyd
London
P065

Tom's experience as executive chef of the Polpo group of restaurants no doubt informed his eponymous restaurant, which channels a sense of joie de vivre in such an effortless way. Drawing influence from across Europe, and with a classical simplicity that can only work with excellent ingredients, Tom's food is ideal for a sunny day when you can feast outdoors with friends.

It's rare to get a full day to enjoy outside – time and weather often conspire against us. But when the moment arises, turn to Tom's recipes. The dishes are flexible enough if numbers swell, and also offer the chance to lazily pick at the food while the sun's out. The same can be said of the drinks, which last well and can be drunk casually throughout a long afternoon.

Lee & Kate Tiernan
Black Axe Mangal
London
P073

I was fortunate to be introduced to husband-and-wife Lee and Kate a couple of years back, but I'd probably encountered them during my regular patronage of St. John Bread & Wine, where Lee was head chef and Kate ran front of house. Since then, they launched Black Axe Mangal together – and damn is it awesome. I mean, what's not to love about a heavy metal kebab shop? Lee's injection of fun didn't stop the food being delicious. His experience with his wood-fired oven both in the restaurant (complete with Kiss insignia!) and in his garden is unparalleled.

The carnal pleasure of charred flavours is something I crave come summer, but I don't want meals and drinks to be heavy. Anything boozy or rich puts an end to the evening too quickly! This fare is the perfect combination of tasty and light, and it's plenty flexible to deal with the likely drop-ins that summer encourages.

Tien Ho
Whole Foods
USA
P093

I've been fortunate to have Tien's cooking on many different occasions: in restaurants he's overseen (he opened Momofuku Ssäm in New York as chef de cuisine, then Má Pêche in the same city, and was also executive chef across the Momofuku group); at events (when he was executive chef at Morgans Hotel Group); and at his home with his amazing family in Austin, Texas. His cooking is always exciting and fresh.

I've only ever been in the US for Thanksgiving once (when Natasha, my sister, lived there), but if it's something I get the chance to repeat, I'm going to try and make the stars align and do it with Tien. His genius turkey recipe takes the stress out of a family gathering, and elevates a simple dish to stratospherically delicious levels. Although this is a riff on a Thanksgiving meal, it's too good to be restricted to once a year, and it's amazing for any gathering. I've supplied the recipe for an easy punch too, so you can spend maximum time with your friends and family.

Mark Birchall & Chet Sharma
Restaurant Moor Hall
Lancashire, UK
P103

The talent, experience and innovation that Mark and Chet share between them makes them a restaurant-running powerhouse. They have spent time at some of the world's best venues (Mark via L'Enclume and El Celler de Can Roca; and Chet via The Fat Duck and Mugaritz, among others), and their experimental expertise has come together beautifully in the grounds of Moor Hall.

But world-class cooking is something that's very hard to bring into the home. Having spent time in kitchens, I know that professional preparation doesn't translate well into a domestic setting. Still, there are times where pulling out the stops is worth it, and a few small tweaks mean you'll end up with something extra special. Paired with an equally impressive cocktail, it's a great way to blow away your guests.

Signe Johansen
'Scandilicious', 'How to Hygge'
P109

I'm of Sinhalese heritage, which means I have a sweet tooth. My mum always has a (wonderful) cake in the house, and without meaning to cast a sweeping statement, this seems to be a habit shared by Norwegians. I met Signe through my also-Norwegian girlfriend Anette, and became friends with her mainly due to her sharp intellect and love of whisky. It was only later revealed to me that she's a wizard baker and has written a brilliant baking book, but also combined her cake wisdom with her studies as an anthropologist for her second book, which is about hygge – good Scandinavian living.

As a lover of tea, I'm more than happy to turn to a cuppa alongside a delicious baked treat. But if you're catching up with friends, some light cocktails create more of an event and make for a welcome twist on a classic afternoon tea.

Mr Lyan and team
White Lyan (RIP), Dandelyan and
all them other things
P117

I think it's evident from my venues, my Instagram, this book and my belly that I love the world of food and drink! It's been part of my life for as long as I can remember, and it remains one of my favourite ways to interact with the world and the people I love. I don't get a chance to cook too often, so I'll use the excuse of an event (or even a work project) to get people together.

I like cooking 'family style' – a big pie, a stew or a dish that people can pass around and pick at, and the recipes I've made for this book have that spirit. They're ideal if you're watching a match/Eurovision/the Olympics – whatever floats your boat! This kind of cooking is easy to scale up, and goes great with cocktails, which is why I've called on some of the Lyan team to make them!

Karan Gokani
Hoppers
London
P139

I was jealous when I heard about the launch of Hoppers – Natasha (my sister) and I had always dreamed of opening a Sri Lankan restaurant. But once I'd experienced the work of the team behind it, it quickly became a place I was glad to just be able to enjoy. Karan and his wife Sunaina are of Indian descent, and even though their knowledge of Sri Lankan cuisine is way beyond mine, they prepare Bombay-style food at home. Their ability to host is unmatched – partly due to the fact they're just so lovely! It's something you can experience in the restaurant as they work every role at different times, and they have instilled their warm approach into all their staff.

Being invited into their home is a wonderful experience, and you can get a taste of that with the enormous Indian feast Karan has shared in this book. It's served family-style, meaning you won't have to spend time plating up. And the drinks are designed to temper the spice, balance the big flavours and fit together seamlessly.

Joan Roca
El Celler de Can Roca
Girona, Spain
P151

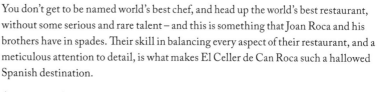

You don't get to be named world's best chef, and head up the world's best restaurant, without some serious and rare talent – and this is something that Joan Roca and his brothers have in spades. Their skill in balancing every aspect of their restaurant, and a meticulous attention to detail, is what makes El Celler de Can Roca such a hallowed Spanish destination.

Attention to detail is just what you need when you're preparing a dish for a date, so don't be scared off by this spectacular, technical dessert. I was fortunate enough to go eat and spend a creative day in the kitchens at El Celler de Can Roca through my friend Daryl who looks after The Macallan whisky, so I've created a wonderful whisky-based cocktail to serve with this patisserie feat.

Tim Siadatan
Trullo, Padella
London
P161

When I first moved (back) to London some years ago, I settled in the lovely area of Canonbury. On my way to first see the flat, I passed Trullo on Highbury Corner and was instantly drawn to the restaurant's intriguingly romantic net-curtained windows. When I dropped in, I was even more enamoured with the food and drinks. Simple, elegant, but executed with such aplomb. Tim and Jordan (Frieda, co-partner) ramped up the excitement when they opened must-visit pasta bar Padella near London Bridge.

Pasta is a versatile ingredient for big and small groups alike (although it took me a while to get past the bad memories it left from my student days). There's something especially comforting about a bowl of the real stuff with a glass of red wine (or a riff-on-wine cocktail) midweek. This dish is spectacular, and perfect for a cosy night in with your partner.

Nuno Mendes
Chiltern Firehouse,
Taberno do Mercado
London
P167

I was excited about Nuno's cooking long before I met him or ate in his restaurants. I'd read plenty about his love of travel and of the way he joined international influences with Portuguese flavours, but this came to life when I went and visited him at the now-closed Viajante. I took my mum for her birthday, and we all have amazing memories from the day (bread course for the win!). The opportunity to enjoy Nuno's vision and skills was not lost with the closing of Viajante though, and thankfully there's now the exquisite Chiltern Firehouse, and the comforting Taberno do Mercado.

Nuno contributed a dish that was all about home comforts to this book. There's a set of delicious recipes that will make you sink into your armchair a little deeper, with drinks to help your drop your shoulders further.

Robin Gill
The Dairy, The Manor,
Paradise Garage, Counter Culture
London
P175

With such amazing restaurants on his CV (The Oak Room, Le Manoir aux Quat'Saisons), Robin's pedigree could easily have led to some very fussy food. But instead it carries all the hallmarks of excellence with a sense of mischief and fun. And it's damn tasty too! I went to The Dairy just after it opened – my sister wouldn't stop insisting I go, even though it was right in the midst of when I was opening my bar Dandelyan. It was the worst possible timing, but two bites in and I was glad I'd taken the evening off.

Every now and then, it's nice to do something a little fancy to wow your friends (without being a total show-off). You don't have to do all the recipes Rob suggests – though it would be enormously impressive if you did – but dip in and try a couple of the fish dishes, together with the sharing cocktails for an exceptional night of dining.

Isaac McHale
The Clove Club
London
P183

Travelling to far-flung countries, and cooking in very different styles of restaurant, Isaac has absorbed a lot of influences. This doesn't mean these cuisines have made their way onto the sensationally good menu at his own restaurant, The Clove Club, but his wide and varied experience can still be felt in subtle ways. His innovative methods and playful takes on favourite dishes makes him such an exciting chef.

His world-class cooking isn't easy to replicate at home, though, so thankfully Isaac has suggested a simple wonton feast perfect for times when you want to chat with friends and let everyone get stuck in without too much effort. I've tried this approach with drinks before, and it's got pretty messy. So here, we've both gone for a structured set-up that allows people to customise the food and drink without it turning into chaos.

Angela Dimayuga
Mission Chinese Food
San Francisco
P189

I'm thankful to have been able to enjoy the peerless food at Danny Bowien's Mission Chinese Food in both its previous and current iterations. Although I'm far too spice-delicate for the real tongue-tingling, mind-melting Szechuan dishes, there's a sense of fun at MCF that everyone can appreciate. This is evident in all of executive chef Angela's cooking. Her attention to the details is fascinating.

Her lightheartedness is carried through in the meal she's designed for this book, which features DIY elements and some playful twists on some retro classics. The drinks take her lead here, with fun, kitsch quirks. It's all very relaxed, but super-delicious!

Lisa Lov
Tigermom
Copenhagen
P197

Jonathan Tam – head chef at Relæ in Copenhagen – was the man behind the awesome aprons we use at my bar Dandelyan, and they were rather charmingly delivered by hand by Jonathan's then sous chef Lisa Lov. We got a chance to hang out and it was clear that it was her drive, joyful spirit and organisation – as well as extraordinary skill – that made her such a brilliant chef. She now has her own place in Copenhagen, Tigermom, blending her heritage, travel and experiences.

For the book, we've created a balance between the dishes and the drinks. Even with my spice-wussness, I think the food is so flavoursome it's worth crying for, but the drinks are designed to take away some of the heat. It's wonderful sharing food, sensational for a giant gathering.

BREAD

with Richard Hart, Tartine Bakery

 +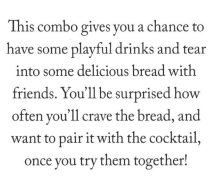

This combo gives you a chance to have some playful drinks and tear into some delicious bread with friends. You'll be surprised how often you'll crave the bread, and want to pair it with the cocktail, once you try them together!

DANDELION MOJITO

Mint-infused rum, dandelion (or gorse) flower, lime, soda

When bottled up, this is super-convenient to serve out. Dandelion flowers are an easy pick while they're in season (and the great thing about weeds is there are plenty of them about). Gorse, marigold or carnations are suitable substitutes that all add a lovely coconut note without being heavy or cloying.

Gather

Makes 1 bottle

1 bottle white or gold rum

1 bunch mint

75g (2½oz) demerara (light brown cane) sugar

2 tbsp dandelion flowers

Half a lime, to serve

Soda, to top

Mint, to garnish

Method

In a jug, infuse the rum with a washed bunch of mint (cut the lower woody stems away, then add to jug, leaves down), sugar and dandelion flowers. Leave for 3 hours. Ensure the sugar is dissolved, then strain and bottle.

To serve, add 2 shots (50ml/2oz) to a glass filled with ice, squeeze in 2 wedges of lime, top with soda and garnish with a sprig of mint.

SPINACH DIP AND FLATBREADS

I moved to California from London nearly ten years ago. At every party across America, without fail, there is a spinach dip. Spinach dip is exactly what you want to slather over your warm bread. I've never seen it in England, so I wanted to share it with you guys who don't live here. I have yet to meet someone that doesn't love it.

As for the flatbreads, I am a baker and there is always bread at my house, so I wanted to make a bread recipe that is easy to make and enjoy with friends and family. I believe in using natural starter, but explaining the hows and whys would take more than one recipe, so with that in mind I've kept it easy and accessible to everyone. But if you have a starter, by all means use it. I have included some ideas for filling the flatbreads, but I haven't given an exact recipe. I would really love for you to be creative and customise it to your taste. *Richard Hart*

Gather

Spinach dip

300g (10½oz/1⅔ cups) cooked, drained, chopped spinach (you can use frozen that has been thawed and drained)

150g (5½oz) chopped water chestnuts

1 bunch of spring onions (scallions), chopped

450g (1lb/3¾ cups) sour cream or crème fraîche

225g (8oz/1 cup) mayonnaise

10g (1⅓ tbsp) garlic powder

20g (3 tbsp) onion powder

5g (1 tbsp) red chilli flakes (optional but it's good with a little kick)

50g (1¾oz/¼ cup) fine-grated parmigiano reggiano

Juice of half a lemon

Stuffed flatbreads (makes 3)

700g (1lb 9oz/5½ cups) plain (all-purpose) flour, plus extra for dusting

300g (10½oz/2⅓ cups) wholemeal (wholewheat) flour

800ml (1½ pints/3¼ cups) water

25g (1oz/1½ tbsp) salt

2½g (¾ tsp) instant dry yeast

Olive oil, for brushing

Filling ideas

Mixed olives; lemon zest and thyme; chorizo, potato and rosemary; roasted pumpkin and pumpkin seeds with marjoram; mixed mushrooms; loads and loads of goat's cheese. Really anything you want. The combinations and possibilities are endless.

Method

For the spinach dip, combine all the ingredients in a bowl. Refrigerate for at least 2 hours. I like to make it a day in advance. The longer it sits, the better the flavour.

For the bread, mix all the ingredients together in a large bowl until the flour is incorporated – it takes about 3–5 minutes. Scrape the sides of the bowl down, cover the bowl with cling film and leave it on your counter for 1 hour. This starts the dough activity. After the first hour, place the bowl in the fridge for at least 12 hours, but 24 is better.

When you are ready to make your bread, preheat the oven to 260°C (500°F/highest possible gas mark).

Put the dough on a lightly floured surface. Using a dough scraper or a knife divide the dough into three equal portions. Push each portion into a square roughly 20 x 20cm (8 x 8 inches) and 2cm (¾ inch) thick. It doesn't need to be exact.

Top each square with the filling of your choice. Be generous but use your own judgment – and leave space around the edges. You need to be able to wrap the dough around the filling. Work your way around the edge of the dough, pulling the edge into the centre, encasing the filling inside the dough. Lightly dust the top of the dough with flour, then lift and lightly flour underneath the dough. Press the dough together to ensure it is sealed and flatten it back to the original 20cm square.

Line a baking sheet with baking paper.

Place the dough on the baking paper and score each one with a series of cuts. The cuts should go all the way through the dough. Then gently pull open the cuts. Rest the dough for 45 minutes in a warm place, such as on top of the oven.

After 45 minutes, brush each loaf with olive oil. Bake in the hot oven for 30–40 minutes until fully baked. The final loaf should be nice and dark. If you are worried about it being underbaked, you can take the internal temperature of the loaf, which should be 92°C (198°F).

FROSÉ MARGARITA

Blanco tequila, lime, rosé vermouth, Peychaud's bitters, wildflower honey

I usually deplore frozen margaritas as they're often made with cheap tequila and pre-made sour mix (which sadly often comes powdered). Here I've embraced the ability of the margarita to get the party going – but I've used real ingredients!

Gather

Serves 5

6 shots (150ml/6oz) blanco tequila

6 shots (150ml/6oz) rosé vermouth

4 shots (100ml/4oz) lime juice

1 tsp Peychaud's bitters

4 shots (100ml/4oz) wildflower honey water (honey mixed 1:1 with warm water)

Limes and amaranth shoots, to garnish

Method

Add everything to a blender with 2 scoops of crushed ice, and blend until smooth. Serve in frozen coupettes with a slice of lime and some red amaranth shoots.

GARDEN BITES

with Nieves Barragán Mohacho, Barrafina

When the sun comes out, you're going to want to pair this sherry-spiked cocktail with the light, bright, Spanish tuna dish by the wonderful Nieves.

CIDER FIX

Amaretto, lemon,
Angostura, cider
(pictured previous page)

Gather

Just under 2 shots (40ml/1.6oz)
Amaretto liqueur

Just under 1 shot (20ml/0.8oz)
lemon juice

2 dashes Angostura bitters

Dry cider, to top

1 lemon with leaves, to garnish

Radishes, to serve

Method

Short shake the liqueur, lemon juice
and bitters with ice, then double strain
over ice into a thin rocks glass and
top with dry, tart cider. Garnish with
a long lemon twist and a lemon leaf,
and serve with radishes and some real
butter to eat them with.

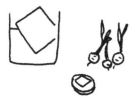

POLLENO

Fino, green apple, honey, fennel pollen

This sour is deliciously light and fresh. The fennel pollen
contrasts really nicely, but garnish with a bright aromatic if
that's unavailable – chamomile, fresh basil or lavender would
all be good options. It's best to juice tart, really green apples
(Granny Smith work well) as they provide the acidity here.
You can use a teaspoon of ascorbic acid (vitamin C – readily
available powdered) for every three apples to keep them nice
and green – just add it straight to the juice as it's pressed.

Gather

2 shots (50ml/2oz) Tio Pepe fino sherry
(en rama when available)

Just over 1 shot (30ml/1oz) freshly
pressed *à la minute* green apple juice

1 tbsp honey water (a citrussy and floral
honey mixed 1:1 with warm water)

1 egg white

Fennel pollen, to garnish

Method

Shake all without ice (aside from the
garnish), shake with cubed ice, then
double strain into a large chilled
coupette. Garnish with some fennel
pollen dusted over the top.

Gather

Just over 2 shots (60ml/2.4oz) amontillado sherry

Just under 1 shot (20ml/0.8oz) lemon juice

10g (½oz) fresh fig leaves

2 shots (50ml/2oz) vodka

200g (7oz) sugar

Soda, to top

Chard and edible flowers, to garnish

RESTED COLLINS

Amontillado, lemon, fig leaf, soda

Method

Fig leaf syrup (makes lots; keep refrigerated):
Fig leaves can be bought dried, and provide a delightful green note that's somewhere between fig and coconut. Finely slice and soak the leaves in the vodka in the fridge for 4 days. On day 4 make a syrup of the white sugar dissolved in 4 shots (100ml/4oz) hot water, then mix in the strained tincture. Keep in a dark, closed container in the fridge.

To serve:
Add the sherry, lemon and just under 1 shot (20ml/0.8oz) fig leaf syrup to a hi-ball filled with ice. Stir, add more ice, then top with soda. Garnish with a stem of chard and flowers.

Method

First make the ajo blanco. Put the bread, almonds, garlic and milk into a large bowl and refrigerate overnight. The next morning, put these ingredients into a blender, along with the grapes, apples and vinegar. Blend well. Slowly add the oil as you blend until a smooth emulsion is formed. Season with salt and pepper to taste.

Cut the tuna loin in half so you have two equal-sized cubes. On a grill pan over a medium heat, sear the tuna loins on each side, but don't let them take on too much colour.

Mix the soy, mirin and sliced ginger. Add the brown sugar so it dissolves. Place the tuna loins in the marinade in a sealed container and refrigerate overnight.

The next day, turn the tuna loins over and leave to marinate overnight again.

To serve, spread the ajo blanco thickly on to a plate, thinly slice the tuna and spread it out on top of the ajo blanco. Drizzle with some of the marinade sauce and some olive oil.

TUNA WITH AJO BLANCO

You'll only need half the ajo blanco for this tuna dish – the rest will keep in the fridge for a week. It's very good served with mackerel, or as a cold soup garnished with grapes and flaked almonds. *Nieves Barragán Mohacho*

Gather

Serves 6

1kg (2lb 4oz) sashimi-grade tuna

200ml (7fl oz/¾ cup) soy sauce

200ml (7fl oz/¾ cup) mirin

3cm (1.1 inch) ginger, thinly sliced

80g (2¾oz/½ cup) brown sugar

½ quantity of ajo blanco (see right)

Drizzle of olive oil, to serve

For the ajo blanco

Half large loaf of white bread

80g (2¾oz/½ cup) whole blanched almonds

1 garlic clove

300ml (10fl oz/1¼ cups) milk

50g (1¾oz) red grapes

3 Granny Smith apples, peeled

25ml (scant 2 tbsp) moscatel vinegar

150ml (5fl oz/⅔ cup) olive oil

Salt and pepper

This isn't about making trash taste delicious (although it can), and it's certainly not about being puritanical – it's about abundant ingredients, and the wasted and forgotten bits you'd never thought to use.

GUILT FREE FEAST

with Douglas McMaster, Silo

CARROT TOP COLLINS

Gin, blackcurrant leaf, lemon, carrot leaf syrup, soda

Carrot leaves/fronds so often end up in the bin, but they add a lovely green and sweet vegetal note to food and drinks alike. Blackcurrant leaves can be bought from specialist suppliers, but they're also easy to pick (just make sure it's legal, and you're not ravaging a private hedgerow!).

Gather

3 shots (75ml/3oz) London dry gin

3 blackcurrant leaves

Fronds from 2 carrots

100g (3½oz) sugar

1 tsp ascorbic acid
(vitamin C powder)

1 shot (25ml/1oz) fresh lemon juice
(save the rind and leaves for Paw
Broon's Whisky Sourz, p45)

Soda, to top

Bitter lettuce leaf, to garnish

Method

Blackcurrant leaf tincture:
Soak 3 blackcurrant leaves in 1 shot (25ml/1oz) of the gin for 1 week. Wring leaves and strain. Keep in a dark bottle in the fridge.

Carrot leaf syrup (makes enough for 6 or so serves):
Take the carrot fronds, and blend with the sugar and 4 shots (100ml/4oz) warm water along with the ascorbic acid – this is easy to buy and helps keep the green vibrancy. If unavailable, plunge the leaves in boiling water for 10 seconds, and refresh immediately in ice-cold water. You can strain this syrup if you want, but the little bits aren't too offensive if you blend it well!

To serve:
Add to a hi-ball filled with ice the remaining 2 shots (50ml/2oz) gin, lemon juice, 3 dashes of the blackcurrant leaf tincture and just under 1 shot (20ml/0.8oz) carrot leaf syrup. Stir, add more ice then crown with soda. Garnish with a leaf of bitter lettuce.

+

POTATOES, BLACKCURRANTS AND WILD CARROT

This is a simple, vibrant dish for the late summer months. Properly grown blackcurrants have a complex, understated flavour that complements young potatoes beautifully. This dish offers up gastronomic diversity with the addition of whey and wild carrots, but there are simple alternatives (see notes). Typically, potatoes this small will be rejected due to industrial farming regulations, with specially designed sieves used so that the little potatoes fall away. *Douglas McMaster*

Notes

Get the best blackcurrants.

Choose potatoes grown in good soil, about the same size as the blackcurrants. The small size is not essential but it does create an equal balance of flavour as you eat.

If you can't source wild carrot flowers, lemon thyme is a fine alternative.

You can get whey from a good cheese shop. Otherwise, use water with a squeeze of lemon juice.

Gather

Serves 4–6

1 litre (1¾ pints/4 cups) whey

400g (14oz) small potatoes

1 litre (1¾ pints/4 cups) water

5g (1 tsp) salt

Approx 100–200g (3½oz–7oz) butter (depending on quantity of reduced whey)

300g (10½oz/3 cups) blackcurrants

10g (¼oz/4 tbsp) wild carrot flowers

Coarse sea salt

Method

Reduce the whey on a low heat until it turns a butterscotch colour, with a strong sweet-and-sour flavour – roughly 20 minutes. You should have about 100–200ml (3½–7fl oz).

Boil the potatoes in the water, with the salt, until tender.

Slowly whisk the butter into the reduced whey over a low-medium heat. Use enough butter to reach a thick consistency that will glaze the potatoes. Add the potatoes and blackcurrants, and adjust the seasoning and acidity if desired (perhaps if the blackcurrants were more jammy or less acidic).

Divide the potatoes and blackcurrants between shallow bowls, garnish with the wild carrot flowers and season with coarse sea salt.

RAW BEEF, FERMENTED BEETROOT COLESLAW AND WILD GARLIC

This is a punchy dish with big, spicy attitude. The intense flavour comes from the two-week fermented beetroot, which works in harmony with the beef. This completely raw dish looks beautiful too, and will not fail to impress. If you have the time, you should definitely make the brown butter to dress the beef. This dish is a great example of maximising resources – using secondary meat cuts such as small cuts (and even trim) that would often get thrown away or used for a lesser purpose. You can also have a 'leapfrog' production process with the beetroot: the first time you make this recipe, you can use your fresh beetroot for anything you like, then ferment the excess. Next time, you'll have a batch of fermented beetroot and be ready to make the next. This way of absorbing waste into fermentation is a beautiful part of a zero-waste philosophy. *D McM*

Gather

Serves 4–6

Approx 10–15 large candy beetroots (beets) (you need enough to produce lots of fresh beetroot discs, fresh coleslaw, plus fermented beetroot – enough to fill a Kilner jar or fermentation crock)

Sea salt

250g (9oz) block of butter (way more than you need but brown butter is an amazingly versatile product that will sit happily in your fridge for ages – use with fish dishes, meat dishes and even on desserts)

200g (7oz) wild garlic

100g (3½oz) parsley sprigs

800ml (1½ pints/3⅓ cups) rapeseed oil

3 eggs

Juice of half a lemon

300g (10½oz) beef muscle, from a happy, grass-fed cow

Coarse sea salt and freshly ground black pepper

10g (¼oz/1 tbsp) salted wild garlic capers (optional)

Method

If you are 'leapfrogging' (ie you already have some fermented beetroot ready), simply prepare your fresh beetroot. Peel the skins off the beetroot and add them to your compost heap. Use a mandolin to slice the beetroot into 1mm (¹⁄₁₆ inch) sheets. Cut 2cm (¾ inch) discs out of the sheets with a cutter or apple corer, set the trim aside – this will make either your first or next batch of fermented beetroot. You also need to coarsely grate fresh beetroot (around 2 tablespoons) for the coleslaw and set it aside for the final dish.

To make the fermented beetroot, weigh the trimmed beetroot (that's what's left after all the fresh discs and grated beetroot have been set aside), then add 2% of its weight in sea salt to the mix.

In a large bowl, massage the salt into the beetroot before squashing it all into a sterilised Kilner jar or fermentation crock. Ideally, you want to fill the jar to the very brim, squashing it down firmly until the 'leached' moisture covers all the solids right to the top. Leave to ferment for between 10 days and 2 weeks.

There will be plenty of excess ferment, which is brilliant eaten on its own as a snack. I always ferment at least ten times as much as I actually need.

To make the brown butter, put the butter into a small pan with a solid base on a low-medium heat. Cook it slowly, until it smells nutty and the sound of crackling stops. Immediately pass it through a fine sieve and reserve. When it cools down, it should be a deep brown colour, smelling nutty and sweet. This can be used to dress anything!

To make a wild garlic oil, blanch the wild garlic and parsley in boiling water for 30 seconds, then plunge into ice water. Drain the herbs extremely well, then put in the blender with half the oil and turn the blender on. After some time, the friction of the blender creates heat, so keep the wild garlic oil blending until the oil reaches 64°C (147°F), then pass through a very fine sieve or cloth.

There will be plenty of excess wild garlic oil, which can be used for a diverse array of dishes from pasta to salads.

Next, make a quick mayonnaise. Crack the eggs into a deep narrow container and hand-blend them with the lemon juice. Then, pour the remaining oil slowly into the egg mixture, blending as you go, so that it emulsifies into a thick mayonnaise. Don't worry about the seasoning, as you will have to season the final coleslaw.

To finish the coleslaw, combine 2 tablespoons of the fermented beetroot with an equal amount of fresh grated beetroot and 1 tablespoon of the mayonnaise. Season to taste.

When you are ready to serve, dice the beef into large chunks. Season the tartare with a touch of the wild garlic oil, a good drizzle of brown butter, a sprinkle of coarse sea salt and a heavy grind of black pepper.

To serve, spoon a tablespoon of the coleslaw on to each plate. Spoon a tablespoon of the tartare on top of the coleslaw. Finally, scatter the discs of fresh beetroot randomly across the dish, and dress with a generous amount of wild garlic oil, a pinch of salt and the wild garlic capers (if using).

PAW BROON'S WHISKY SOURZ

Whiskies, compost shrub, lemon shell, egg and chocolate sugar

This is a whisky sour I originally created so busy friends didn't need specialist equipment or complicated prep – but it evolved into this slightly more involved but delicious sharing serve.

Gather

Serves 2

30g (1oz) soft, leftover berries

5g (¼oz) fruit and veg peelings (apples, carrots, parsnips, beets are all good)

4 shots (100ml/4oz) cider vinegar

1 tsp chocolate powder

9 tsp unrefined sugar

3 shots (75ml/3oz) whisky blend – made from blending together the leftover scant shots of whisky at the bottom of bottles

1 egg, including shell

1 half lemon husk (saved after being juiced in Carrot Top Collins, p39)

5 ice cubes

Lemon leaves, to garnish

Method

Compost shrub:
Throw soft berries on the turn along with the fruit and veg peelings into the cider vinegar. Put on to the hob in a pan and cook over a medium heat for 15 minutes until reduced by half. Cool and strain.

Chocolate sugar:
Mix the chocolate powder with the unrefined sugar and keep aside.

To serve:
To a blender or Nutribullet, add the whisky, 1 tablespoon compost shrub, 1½ tablespoons chocolate sugar, the lemon rind, the egg (wash first, but just chuck the whole thing in, shell and all!) and the ice. Blend well until smooth, then strain using a sieve over ice in two rocks glasses. Garnish with scored leaves from the lemon.

James's food and drink have a simplicity to them. To really make them shine, I propose pushing the boat out and buying the best ingredients around (with both the booze and food!). This is the kind of meal that you can draw friends in with!

THE COUNTRY TABLE

with James Lowe, Lyle's

HAYMAKER

Seedlip Garden, pearl barley, Starkrimson pear, ling honey, soda

This non-alcoholic cocktail (using sugar- and alcohol-free spirit Seedlip Garden) is crisp and adult, and an amazing palate refresher before a meal, or alongside some light bites!

Gather

2 Starkrimson or Seckel pears (red-skinned, crisp and floral varieties)

100g (3½oz) pearl barley

1 shot (25ml/1oz) Seedlip Garden

1 tsp ling honey

Soda, to top

Method

Pearl barley water (makes enough for 10 or so serves):
Slice 300g (10½oz) of the pear then add to a large pot with 700ml (1¼ pints) water and the pearl barley. Bring to the boil and simmer for 20 minutes. Allow to cool, then press through a sieve.

To serve:
Add to a shaker the Seedlip Garden, 1 shot (25ml/1oz) pearl barley water and the honey. Stir to dissolve the honey, then add ice, short shake and double strain into a flute. Add a slice of pear, then top with chilled soda water.

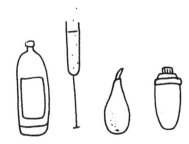

My favourite way to start any meal is with a few bites, normally something salty or punchy to get the taste buds going. The following all have that going on and they encapsulate my approach to food. Just note, the goose ham needs a month to cure. These recipes make a feast for six people. *James Lowe*

OYSTERS AND RHUBARB

Gather

6 rhubarb sticks

20g (¾oz/1⅔ tbsp) caster (superfine) sugar

12 native oysters

2½cm (1 inch) fresh horseradish

Crème fraîche, to serve

Method

Chop two sticks of the rhubarb into small dice. Juice the rest and bring to the boil. When boiling, add the sugar, stir and leave to cool. When the juice cools to 60°C (140°F), pour over the diced rhubarb and leave to cool completely. Shuck the oysters. Peel and shave the horseradish into thin slivers. Mix the desired amount through the rhubarb and serve on top of the oysters, with a little blob of crème fraîche, or leave people to decide how much horseradish they want to add!

GOOSE HAM

Gather

4 goose (or duck) breasts

400g (14oz/1⅔ cups) salt

100g (3½oz/⅔ cup) demerara (light brown cane) sugar

Method

Trim the silver skin off the goose breasts and trim the fat to the edge of the meat. Mix the salt and the sugar together. Weigh each breast individually. Season the breast with an amount of the salt/sugar mix equal to 5% of the weight of the breast. Wrap it in cling film tightly and place in the fridge for 24 hours. Flip the breast and leave for another 24 hours. After that, remove from the cling film, give it a quick rinse under cold water and pat dry. Tie with string and hang in a cool ventilated place for four weeks, until the grouse ham firms up completely.

ANCHOVIES AND CITRUS

Gather

1 tin best anchovies

1 yuzu

1 lime

2 clementines

1 Meyer lemon

Olive oil

Method

Zest the fruit into a container and cover with the best olive oil you can find. Strain the anchovies and lay out on a plate, with enough time for them to come to room temperature. Cover with the zest and oil mix.

PINT OF ENGLISH

Cider brandy, pale ale, rhubarb, sour cherry, crab apple

This is an amazing group serve, made as a pint for four. Like an ale, it's best alongside rich dishes, and has just the right amount of fruitiness to match a main. Try to find a light pale ale – you need some hoppy bitterness, but nothing that's going to overpower.

Gather

Serves 4

100g (3½oz) sliced rhubarb

100g (3½oz) white sugar

4 shots (100ml/4oz) 5yo Somerset cider brandy

3 shots (75ml/3oz) tart cherry juice

2 shots (50ml/2oz) cloudy apple juice

2 tsp crab apple jelly

8 shots (200ml/8oz) chilled pale ale, to top

Candied crab apples, to garnish

Method

Rhubarb syrup:
Add the rhubarb and sugar to a pan with 4 shots (100ml/4oz) water. Gently poach for a few minutes until the rhubarb is soft. Allow to cool, then pass through a sieve, pressing all liquid from the fruit.

To serve:
Add to a shaker the cider brandy, just over 2 shots (60ml/2.4oz) of the rhubarb syrup, the cherry and apple juices and the apple jelly. Shake with ice, then strain into a small jug and top with the ale. Serve in rocks glasses filled with ice and garnish with candied crab apples (or slices of apple).

MUSSELS, CIDER AND LOVAGE

I love mussels because they are so quick and easy to cook and leave you with such a good stock. Nothing tastes more 'of the sea' than mussel cooking liquid. This recipe is slightly more involved than simply dropping the mussels in a pot, but all the better for it. Lovage and sweet and sour from the reduced cider have become a bit of a classic combination for me at Lyle's. *JL*

Gather

300g (10½oz) lovage

600ml (20fl oz/2½ cups) grapeseed oil

3kg (6½lb) mussels

350ml (12fl oz/1½ cups) cider

30g (1oz) lemon thyme sprigs

200g (7oz/¾ cup) butter

Method

In a high-powered blender, blend the lovage and the oil until it gets hot (60°C/140°F). At that point, the purée that has formed will split – the oil and solids will separate. When this happens, pour the mixture into a strainer lined with muslin with a container underneath and move to the fridge to strain and cool.

Clean the mussels by scraping the shells and pulling any 'beards' from the shells. Set half the mussels aside to serve. In a heavy-based pan with a lid, combine the remaining mussels, cider and lemon thyme sprigs. Turn the heat up to full and put a lid on the pan. After 3 minutes, check the mussels – you want them all to open. Turn the heat down, give them a stir and let the mix cook out without the lid for a couple of minutes. Turn off the heat, put the lid

back on and leave for 10 minutes. Pour the mussels through a strainer to collect the stock created. Reduce this liquid by half, until the liquid is quite strong and salty. Measure the liquid – you want about 400ml (14fl oz/1⅔ cups). (If you have too much liquid left at the end of cooking, save it for a soup – it will need to be let down a little.)

In a high-powered blender, blitz the 400ml liquid, 150g (5½oz) of the cooked mussels and the butter.

When you're ready to serve the dish, return the mussel liquid mix to the pan and add the remaining uncooked mussels. Cook for about 3 minutes until the mussels open.

Put a spoonful of the lovage oil in each serving bowl and then pour in the mussels and the cooking liquid.

BITTER LEAF SALAD

Gather

4 blood oranges

1 Cédrat lemon

1 lemon

300g (10½oz) Italian bitter leaves (tardivo, radicchio, grumolo, treviso)

Method

Peel three of the blood oranges and segment them so there is no pith. Save all the juice created when you do this. Slice the Cédrat lemon very thinly – you're aiming for at least 18 slices, a few per person. Blanch the lemon slices in boiling water for 5 seconds. Take out and dress with the saved orange juice and a little olive oil. Juice the remaining blood orange and the lemon, measure and then mix with equal parts olive oil to make a vinaigrette. Just before serving, toss the leaves, blood orange segments and lemon slices with the vinaigrette and a decent pinch of salt. The leaves are bitter and quite hardy so can take a little more seasoning than usual. Depending on what's in season, you could substitute them for succulent cabbages (like kale) or Japanese leaves (komatsuna).

BEEF RIB

This is the sort of thing I love to eat at home. Where the meat comes from is incredibly important. Consider every link in the chain: the breed, the farmer, the age of the animal, how it is stored and aged, and finally how it is cooked. If all the links are as good, then you can end up with something really beautiful that looks very simple. *JL*

Gather

2 fore rib steaks (about 700g/1lb 9oz each)

50g (1¾oz) flat-leaf parsley leaves

50g (1¾oz) tarragon leaves

50g (1¾oz) chervil leaves

4 mint leaves

150ml (5fl oz/⅔ cup) olive oil, plus extra for brushing

30g (1oz) anchovies, chopped to almost a paste

1 garlic clove, finely grated

20g (¾oz/4 tsp) Dijon mustard

30g (1oz) fine capers

30ml (2 tbsp) red wine vinegar

Coarse sea salt and freshly ground black pepper

Method

A couple of hours before you want to cook the beef, season well with coarse salt and leave it out of the fridge.

When you are ready to cook, preheat the oven to 100°C (210°F/gas mark ¼). Place a heavy-duty ovenproof pan on the stove and let it get very hot. Brush the beef with olive oil and place in the pan. Brown the meat on all sides. Flip the beef every 30 seconds until it has an even colour and crust all over. Transfer to the oven and continue to cook for about 10 minutes, or until you reach a core temperature of 52°C (125°F). Take the beef out and rest for 5 minutes before serving.

Very finely chop all the herbs by hand and combine them together in a bowl, then add the olive oil. Getting the herbs covered in oil quickly keeps them looking bright and tasting fresh, and stops them from oxidising and changing flavour. Add the anchovies, grated garlic, mustard and capers to the herbs. Stir and season with salt and pepper to taste. Just before serving, add the red wine vinegar to taste. The green sauce should be salty, acidic, mustardy – it's a condiment so make it punchy!

PEAR, OATS AND BERKSWELL

This is quite a non-sweet dessert, a trademark at Lyle's!
It features my favourite fruit: pears are generally sold underripe,
but leave for a few days and they'll become truly special. *JL*

Gather

10 best-quality pears (British Reds, Comice, Passe-Crassane), extremely ripe (see method)

Sorbet stabiliser

300g (10½oz/1⅓ cups) butter, soft

265g (9¼oz/1¾ cups) demerara (light brown cane) sugar

200g (7oz/2½ cups) oats

10g (¼oz/2 tsp) bicarbonate of soda (baking soda)

10g (¼oz/2 tsp) salt

Berkswell cheese

Sea salt, to serve

Method

Leave the pears and a bunch of bananas in a container, uncovered, at room temperature for a week or until the pears are very ripe and very soft. Ideally, you're looking for the point when they're about to start fermenting. Blend the pears (including skin) and measure the sugar content of the purée with a refractometer – you are looking for 20. If it's under, add sugar to get it to 20 (If you don't have a refractometer but the pears are perfectly ripe, it should be okay.) Weigh the purée and add 20g (¾oz) of sorbet stabiliser per 1kg (2lb 4oz) of purée. Blend for 2 minutes. Pass the mix through a strainer and freeze.

Beat the butter and sugar until pale and creamy (I use a KitchenAid with a paddle for 1 minute). Fold in the oats, bicarbonate of soda and measured salt with a spoon and leave to rest for 1 hour.

Roll out the mix in between layers of baking paper until 3mm (⅛ inch) thick. Transfer the rolled-out biscuit mix, with the paper, to a heavy, flat baking tray. Lay another baking tray on top and bake at 160°C (325°F/gas mark 3) for 10 minutes, until it is golden brown. Take out and leave to cool on a cloth.

When the sorbet is frozen and you're ready to serve, spoon the desired amount into a bowl in an even layer. Cover with the oat biscuits and thin shavings of Berkswell. Finish with a small sprinkle of sea salt. The idea is that in every mouthful you will get a bit of everything.

PUNCH & JUDY

Navy-ish rum and 'walnut ketchup'

This is a twist on an old port-based liqueur I discovered years back. I've made a twist to include some intense fish sauce – this might sound weird, but get some of the high-grade stuff (it's usually for dipping) and it adds a rich background spice with just the right amount of funk to it!

Gather

250ml (10oz) port

12g (¼oz) walnuts

½ tsp fennel seed

½ tsp peppercorns

4g (¼oz) sliced ginger

1 bay leaf

40g (1½oz) chopped dates

150g (5½oz) sugar

Just under 1 shot (20ml/0.8oz) cider vinegar

1 tsp 40N fish sauce

2 tsp light Cuban rum

2 tsp golden Bajan rum

2 tsp dark Jamaican rum

Lemon peel, to garnish

Method

Walnut ketchup (makes a small bottle):
Add to a pan the port, walnuts, fennel seed, pepper, ginger, bay leaf, dates, sugar and cider vinegar. Boil all for 5 minutes on high heat. Allow to cool then add the fish sauce. Mix, strain, bottle and keep in the fridge.

To serve:
Add to a mixing glass the rums and 2 teaspoons walnut ketchup. Stir with ice then strain into cocktail glasses. Snap over a small lemon twist and discard it.

The drinks here won't knock you out, and they really suit being drunk outside as they hold for a good number of hours allowing you to graze and top up drinks as and when. Just find a sunny spot and spend the whole day enjoying this wonderful fare.

ALFRESCO PARTY

with Tom Oldroyd, Oldroyd

INSTA-VERMOUTH & SODA

Red wine, white wine, cognac, spices, raspberry syrup, soda

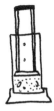

I first made this drink years back as part of a competition, then quickly realised how useful it was for using up open bottles of wine and serving at home! It's best with a lighter red (think Nero d'Avola) and a zesty white (like a Picpoul).

Gather

1 shot (25ml/1oz) red wine

1 shot (25ml/1oz) white wine

1 tbsp cognac

Pinch wormwood

1 clove

1 cardamom pod

Pinch cacao nib

Pinch loose-leaf tea

Pinch dried oregano

Slice of fresh ginger

1 tbsp raspberry syrup

3 dashes orange bitters

Soda, to top

Lemon peel and edible flowers, to garnish

Method

Add wines, cognac, spices and tea to an Aeropress or a small jug, and leave to infuse (ideally for 5 minutes) while you prepare the other elements.

Add raspberry syrup to a wine glass with orange bitters, then plunge the Aeropress into the glass, or filter contents from the jug using a coffee filter.

Fill with ice, then top with soda and garnish with a strip of lemon peel and some edible flowers.

Note: this makes enough for one serve, but an Aeropress can hold enough for several serves at once, so scale up as needed.

WHOLE ROAST MACKEREL, POTATO AND RED ONION SALAD

I fell in love with food at a young age and I'd be browsing the local farmers' market while my friends played football. I remember for one post-match meal I made them roast Surrey Hills venison and 'ribbons' of carrot with a wine reduction!

Oldroyd restaurant serves simple, European, classic comfort food. I like to think of it as holiday food done properly. When it comes to alfresco dining, there's little more I enjoy than some simply grilled blue fish. Accompanied by the waxy starch of a potato salad, the pepperiness of rocket and the cool fresh snap of beans and sweet tomatoes, it really takes some beating.

Although collecting these ingredients from the markets of a coastal Mediterranean town on the same day they were caught or picked – and then eating them as the sun sets, after a day at the beach – is the ideal scenario, it is not compulsory.

Tom Oldroyd

Method

In a wide pan, cover the potatoes (in their skins) with cold salted water. Bring to the boil and very gently simmer for 30 minutes or until just tender when skewered with a sharp knife. It is important not to boil the pan too vigorously. Gently gently.

Put the sliced red onion in a small bowl and sprinkle over a little salt. Leave for 10 minutes to soften and remove any bitterness.

With a slotted spoon, remove the potatoes and leave to cool slightly before slicing into thick (1cm/½ inch) rounds. Place in a large mixing bowl and season while still warm with a good amount of olive oil, a little vinegar, salt and pepper. Add the sliced red onion and the rocket, which should wilt slightly. Put the salad to one side.

Fire up the BBQ or set your grill to medium.

Pat the mackerel dry and season with salt, pepper and a little olive oil. Grill on a medium heat for roughly 3 minutes on each side or until the flesh loses its bounce when touched.

To serve, place some of the potatoes on each plate with a mackerel on top.

Gather

Serves 6

2kg (4lb 8oz) medium-sized Desiree potatoes (it's important to use these red-skinned, waxy potatoes, and make sure they're all a similar size so they cook evenly)

1 medium red onion, thinly sliced

Good-quality olive oil

Good-quality red wine vinegar

Sea salt and freshly ground black pepper

1 large handful of washed rocket leaves

6 small (or 3 large) fresh mackerel, gutted and scaled by your fishmonger

Serves 6

4 large ox heart tomatoes

250g (9oz) runner beans

A small handful of picked
oregano leaves

Good-quality olive oil

Good-quality red wine vinegar

Sea salt and freshly
ground black pepper

OX HEART TOMATOES, RUNNER BEANS AND OREGANO

Method

Fill and boil a kettle. Make a little cross incision in the base of each tomato. Place in a large bowl and pour over the boiling water, covering all the tomatoes. Leave for 30 seconds and then carefully remove from the water and peel away the skins. Trim the sides of the runner beans with a peeler to remove the stringy parts. Cut on the diagonal at 2½cm (1 inch) intervals and blanch in a pan of simmering salted water for 3 minutes. Remove and place in iced water to refresh.

To construct the tomato salad, simply slice up the ox heart tomatoes and place in a mixing bowl with the runner beans. Sprinkle in the oregano leaves. Season with olive oil, a little red wine vinegar, salt and pepper. Toss together and transfer to a serving bowl in the middle of the table for everyone to help themselves.

+

PEARLY NEGRONI

Lemon gin, Lillet Blanc, Kamm & Sons, grapefruit soda

This is brilliant as a light, white negroni, but to serve it as an outside treat, bottle it up and serve with a bright citrus soda or fresh lemonade to lengthen.

Gather

Makes 1 bottle

300ml (12oz) London dry gin

1 organic lemon

6 shots (150ml/6oz) Lillet Blanc

8 shots (200ml/8oz) Kamm & Sons (or a gentian liqueur if unavailable)

Chilled cans or bottles of grapefruit soda, to top

1 mandarin or any aromatic citrus, to garnish

Method

Infuse the gin with the zest of the lemon for 2 hours, then strain.

Mix the lemon gin with Lillet Blanc and Kamm & Sons, then bottle.

Serve with small cups, ice and slices of mandarin. Pour just under 2 shots (40ml/1.6oz) into cups then top with grapefruit soda and garnish with a slice of mandarin.

BBQs are all about the carnal pleasure of burning stuff (in a controlled way) and being outdoors. Lee has nailed the balance between the elements of the meal that can be made in advance, and other parts to be imbued with smoke on the spot (his feast should serve about eight people). I've taken his lead and suggested some charred ingredients for the drinks, but these can easily be done in advance too (under the grill) to give you maximum time relaxing in the sun.

BBQ

with Lee & Kate Tiernan, Black Axe Mangal

GRILLED PEACH COLLINS
Bourbon, peach and peach bitters, lemon and soda

Giving peaches a quick char on the BBQ balances their heady lusciousness with caramel sweetness and bitter notes. They form more of a garnish here, but the aroma they bring is amazing and they're delicious to eat as you sip and chat. It's a drink that's easily built in the glass – just make each one as people arrive so they don't go flat.

Gather

Just over 1 shot (30ml/1oz) bourbon

1 tbsp Lillet Blanc

2 dashes peach bitters (optional)

1 shot (25ml/1oz) lemon juice

1 tbsp sugar syrup

2 peaches, to garnish (this makes enough for several drinks; use any leftover in the Oolong Soda, p88)

1 stem mint, to garnish

Soda, to top

Method

Grilled peach:
Halve the peaches and remove the stone. Place on a grill above medium coals, or under a medium-high grill. Start to char, and when they've taken some colour and start to look (more!) golden and smell sweeter, remove and cool. When cool, slice into wedges.

To serve:
Fill a small hi-ball with ice, add a slice of the grilled peach, then add all the other ingredients (except the mint and soda) and stir. Add more ice, then top with soda. Garnish with another slice of grilled peach and a sprig of mint.

JEREZANINO
Fino, Aperol, basil and tonic

Gather

2 slices orange

1 shot (25ml/1oz) fino or amontillado sherry

1 shot (25ml/1oz) Aperol

Fever-Tree tonic water, to top

2 green olives, to garnish

1 sprig basil, to garnish

Method

Fill a wine glass with ice, then add a slice of orange, the sherry and Aperol. Add more ice, then top with chilled tonic. Garnish with another slice of orange, the olives and the sprig of basil.

SARDINES GRILLED WITH DULSE SAMBAL

This is by no means an authentic recipe – it's bloody tasty though. It's hard to resist the aroma of oily fish on the grill, when a little fish juice seeps on to the charcoal and this wafts smoke back on to the fish, sending everyone's appetites into a frenzy. *Lee Tiernan*

GRILLED SWEETCORN AND FERMENTED SHRIMP BUTTER

Gather

1 level tbsp fermented shrimp paste

150g (5½oz/⅔ cup) unsalted butter, at room temperature

4 sweetcorn cobs

Method

Mix the shrimp paste into the butter till fully incorporated.

Boil the sweetcorn for 6 minutes. Cut the corn widthways into two chunks. Grill till charred to your liking.

Toss in the shrimp butter and serve.

Gather

1–2kg (2lb 4oz–4lb 8oz) sardines, gutted and scaled (your fishmonger will be happy to do this for you)

Half large cucumber, sliced as thin as you can

1 bunch of coriander (cilantro)

1 bunch of Thai basil

Salt

For the dulse sambal

6 tomatoes (taste may vary depending on the time of year)

6 garlic cloves

3 bird's eye chillies (if you don't like it spicy, use milder or fewer chillies)

1 tbsp shrimp paste

1 tsp dried dulse (optional)

Juice of 2–3 limes

Dried shrimps (optional)

Method

First make the sambal.

Place the tomatoes, garlic, chillies, shrimp paste and dulse in a blender and pulse till smooth. Add the lime juice to taste.

If using the dried shrimp, gently fry till just crisp. Spoon on to a plate covered with kitchen towel to soak up the excess oil.

Salt the sardines and grill on both sides. Let the fish cook for a good minute on the first side – if you try and turn them too early, you run the risk of the skin sticking and ripping. A reliable indication of when they're cooked is when their eyes turn white.

When cooked, place on a platter, cover with the sliced cucumber and pour the sambal over the top. Scatter with the herbs and the fried shrimps (if using), and serve.

Gather

Makes 1 pitcher

1 pineapple

150g (5½oz) sugar

4 stems tarragon

350ml (14oz) cider vinegar

300ml (12oz) reposado tequila

4 shots (100ml/4oz) lime juice

Soda, to top

Small pineapple and soda, to serve

PIÑA PITCHER

Reposado tequila, pineapple and tarragon shrub, lime and soda

A shrub is essentially a cordial made with a base of vinegar and is a useful way of preserving fruits. The acidity of a shrub cuts through richer food. It takes a little planning (make it a week ahead, or as soon as you anticipate some good weather on the horizon), but it'll keep well in the fridge.

Method

Shrub (makes enough for 2 pitchers):
Peel, core and slice a ripe pineapple and place in a mason jar with the sugar and 4 stems of tarragon. Cover with vinegar and stir well. Allow to rest in a cool, dark place for between 2 days and a week, agitating regularly. When ready – it should smell fruity and aromatic – transfer it all to a pan, bring to a rolling boil for 5 minutes, then cool and strain. Keep in a clean bottle in the fridge.

To serve:
Slice small pineapple and grill on the BBQ then allow to cool.

Fill a pitcher with large cubes of ice, add a few slices of charred pineapple then add 4 shots (100ml/4oz) of the shrub, the tequila and the lime juice.

Stir, taste, then fill with more ice and cap with soda. Serve in rocks glasses filled with ice and garnished with sliced strawberries.

Gather

Makes 1 punch bowl

3 mandarins (plus one to garnish)

200g (7oz) real runny honey such as clover or wildflower

5g (1 tsp) Rare Tea Company Cloud Tea

12 dashes Spanish bitters

300ml (12oz) Belvedere Pink Grapefruit

1 bottle (330ml) Gosnell's London mead (or a rich lager)

2 passionfruit and edible flowers, to garnish

HONEY & BURNT HONEY PUNCH

Belvedere Pink Grapefruit vodka, burnt honey, mandarin, tea and mead

Punches are perfect to serve to a group of friends, and allow them to help themselves at a relaxed setting like a BBQ. The toasted notes in this punch are great with the smoky food, but it's got enough brightness to make sure it doesn't all get too heavy. You can burn the honey on the hob, but the smoky edge from the fire is better. I've also specified the Pink Grapefruit maceration from Belvedere, as well as Rare Tea Co's Cloud Tea, but play around with flavours and teas.

Method

Burnt honey tea:
Peel 3 of the mandarins and retain the fruit. Add peel to a metal container and cover with the honey. Place on BBQ and caramelise for about 15 minutes – till the honey begins to bubble, reduce and smell rich. Allow to cool.

Brew the tea in 400ml (14fl oz) of water at 85°C/185°F for 2 minutes, then strain over the cooled honey. Stir to dissolve, then allow to cool. When cold, remove the mandarin peel.

To serve:
Add a large piece of ice to a punch bowl then add the burnt honey tea water, bitters, vodka and the juice of the 3 mandarins. Stir well then garnish with the halved passionfruits, slices of mandarin and edible flowers. Before serving, add the mead, then ladle into cups filled with ice.

LAMB HEART BULGUR

Buying lamb hearts is fairly easy. What is more tricky is getting them prepped and ready for the BBQ. If you're on friendly terms with your butcher, they may trim the hearts for you, but it takes a little time so you might have to roll your sleeves up and do it yourself. It's not as intimidating as you might think and lamb hearts are relatively inexpensive, so if you balls one or two up, it's no biggie. To avoid accidents, make sure you have a sharp knife. If you don't, buy some lamb chops and don't bother trying to tackle the hearts. *LT*

Gather

6 lamb hearts

3 garlic cloves, thinly sliced

1 thyme sprig

1 large red onion, thinly sliced

200ml (7fl oz/¾ cup) red wine vinegar

3 medium brown onions, peeled and halved

Yogurt (in a squeezy bottle if you want to be fancy)

1 tbsp sumac

1 tsp chilli flakes

Vegetable oil

Salt

For the bulgur

300g (10½oz/1⅓ cups) wholewheat bulgur

1 large brown onion, diced

3 tbsp finely chopped preserved lemons

2 tbsp superfine capers or chopped capers

Fistful of chopped flat-leaf parsley

3 tbsp pomegranate molasses

Couple of handfuls of rocket or watercress

Method

First, prepare the hearts. The idea is to end up with thin slivers of heart. Start by placing a heart on a chopping board and trim the fatty part off the top. Remove the membrane from the outside while you're at it. Removing the membrane prevents the meat from curling when you grill it.

You will see that the heart has two chambers. One is bigger than the other. The smaller chamber will make one sliver – separate this and place in a bowl. Cut the bigger chamber through one side so you can open it up into one large piece. You'll notice there is a stringy membrane on the inside – you will have to remove this too. Discard the trim as you go. Slice the meat on an angle into two even pieces.

See? Easy.

Repeat with the other hearts.

Once you've finished trimming and slicing, the hearts are ready to marinate. Drizzle a little oil into the bowl and add the garlic and the thyme. You can do this a couple of days in advance to save yourself any stress when the time comes to cook for your friends.

When the day comes, start by marinating the sliced red onion in the vinegar and lighting the BBQ. The BBQ has to be ripping hot to cook the hearts, so don't dawdle.

Now cook the bulgur. Most of the time, instructions on the side of the packet are pretty accurate. I rinse all the starch off first in a few changes of water before cooking. This prevents the bulgur from clumping together. Heat a good glug of oil in a pan with a lid and sweat the diced onion with a pinch of salt. Add the bulgur and stir into the onions. Once mixed, top up with water till just about covered and bring up to the boil. When it's hit the boil, season to taste, turn off the heat and cover with a tight-fitting lid. Use tin foil if you don't have a lid – just make sure it's tight. Leave for around 20 minutes.

The bulgur will stay warm for a while. The 20 or so minutes it takes for the bulgur to cook gives you plenty of time to prepare the rest of the ingredients. Once the bulgur comes off the boil, you can grill the onion halves.

Lightly oil the onion halves, add a sprinkling of salt and place on the BBQ. You want the onions to colour deeply, but also to cook through a bit, so place them around the sides of the BBQ where the heat is less ferocious. Don't attempt to move these onions before they are ready to be moved. Be patient and don't fiddle. They are ready when they are ready – don't be afraid to get them good and black.

So. Lamb is sliced. Red onion is pickling, bulgur is cooking, onions are on the grill.

Back to the bulgur when it's ready. In a big bowl, mix the preserved lemons, capers and parsley into the bulgur, along with the pomegranate molasses. Finally, add the greens. Arrange on a serving platter.

Remove the now done, gloriously charred onions from the BBQ and add them to the platter.

Toss the lamb heart in salt. Grill the hearts on the hottest part of the grill. If your BBQ is small, cook in batches. If you cook the heart for too long it will become tough. Try a slice or two to get your timings right. You owe it to yourself after all the hard work you put into prepping the meat.

Once the meat is cooked, let it rest on the warm bulgur, which soaks up all the lamb juices. Squirt the yogurt liberally over the meat and sprinkle with sumac and chilli. Scatter the pickled onions on top and serve.

For the curry

12 long red chillies

Caster (superfine) sugar

250ml (9fl oz/1 cup) rice wine vinegar

300g (10½oz) ginger

100g (3½oz) galangal,
tough stems trimmed

16 garlic cloves

100g (3½oz) turmeric root, peeled

10 shallots

150g (5½oz/⅔ cup) unsalted butter

6–8 kaffir lime leaves, fresh

3 lemongrass sticks

3 x 400ml (14fl oz) tins good-quality
coconut milk

Palm sugar, to taste

3 limes

Fish sauce, to taste

2 mangoes

1 large pineapple

1 bunch of coriander
(cilantro), roughly chopped

Salt

For the rice

500g (1lb 2oz/2⅓ cups) basmati rice

2 cinnamon sticks

6 star anise

10 cardamom pods

PINEAPPLE CURRY AND FRAGRANT RICE

This is quite a thin curry, with the fruit added at the end (rather than during cooking). And there are no limits to what you can flavour your rice with. I prefer larger spices such as cinnamon sticks, star anise and cardamom pods, because they are easy to pick out and they go well together. But feel free to express yourself. *LT*

Method

Start by cutting up six of the red chillies. Sprinkle liberally with caster sugar and marinate in the rice vinegar. This can be done days ahead. But an hour or so will get you close if you're being spontaneous.

Blitz the ginger, galangal, garlic, turmeric, shallots and remaining chillies in a blender until you have a smooth paste, add a splash of water if needs be. (Unless you have a very powerful blender, it's a good idea to chop the ginger and galangal before you blitz to help remove the long fibres in the galangal that won't break down during cooking.) Heat the butter in a deep pan and add the paste. Cook for 20 minutes on a medium heat, being careful not to let the paste catch too much. Then, add a pinch of salt and the lime leaves, lemongrass and coconut milk. Simmer for a further 20–25 minutes.

Taste the curry at this point. I add palm sugar, lime juice and fish sauce till I achieve the flavour I'm after. I love fermented, funky fish flavours, so I tend to add more fish sauce than most people. Acid from the lime brings the balance and the sugar sweetens the bitterness of the paste – though taste your fruit first

to check how sweet it is, and be judicious with the palm sugar.

Next, cook the rice. Rinse it until the water runs clean. Put in a pan and just about cover the rice with water. Season with salt, and add the cinnamon, star anise and cardamom pods and bring to the boil. Once the rice comes up to the boil, put a lid on the pan and cook on the lowest heat you have for 12–15 minutes. This is called the absorption method. You should end up with fantastically fluffy rice. You can always follow the instructions on the packet if sceptical.

While the rice is cooking, prepare the mango and pineapple. Cut the mango however you like. The pineapple is best for me simply sliced. Lightly oil and salt the pineapple before applying to the BBQ. Let the pineapple char before moving it as it will stick. Let the sugar caramelise. One side is enough for me.

Place all the fruit on a serving platter and top with the coriander and the pickled chillies.

The curry and the rice can be spooned over from the pot. Enjoy.

Gather

Gather

2 yellow peaches

6g oolong tea leaves

1 shot (25ml/1oz) orgeat

Soda, to top

Method

Grill then slice some yellow peaches (see p74 for full method).

Add the oolong tea leaves to a jug and fill with 300ml (12oz) cold water. Infuse for two hours, then strain. Add the orgeat to the mix and stir.

Pour 5 shots (125ml/5oz) of this mix over cubed ice in a hi-ball, then top with soda. Stir with, then garnish with, a slice of grilled peach.

OOLONG SODA

Almond, oolong, peach and soda

Having some non-alcoholic cocktails is a good idea on long hot days, and also when you have younger ones in tow. The drinks can be decidedly adult in complexity though. This twist on an iced tea uses the same grilled peaches as the Grilled Peach Collins (on p74), but pairs very differently with cold brewed tea and almond syrup.

SORREL COOLER

Hibiscus, watermelon and sage

Gather

10g (0.4oz) dried hibiscus

Stick of cinnamon

Honey, to taste

Watermelon, to garnish

Sage, to garnish

A hibiscus soda is one of the non-alcoholic drinks White Lyan made for Lee and Kate at Black Axe Mangal – the acidity is ideal for cutting through rich dishes. It's also a tip of the hat to the hibiscus drink named sorrel served alongside food in Jamaica and Trinidad (which doesn't contain sorrel the leaf!).

Method

Infuse dried hibiscus and half a stick of cinnamon in 500ml (20oz) cold water for 4–6 hours, then strain. Add honey to taste.

Fill a rocks glass with cubed ice and fill with the hibiscus and cinnamon infusion. Garnish with two slices of watermelon and a sprig of sage.

 +

Get a group together on
a cold day, and this easy
style of food and drink
makes for one fun evening,
whether it's Thanksgiving
or not.

THANKSGIVING
DINNER

with Tien Ho, Whole Foods

LYAN MARY

Vodka, nuked sherry, miso, tomato

Gather

15g (½oz) sweet white miso

4 shots (100ml/4oz) Lea & Perrins Worcestershire sauce (really!)

500ml (20oz) passata

500ml (20oz) tomato juice

½ tsp Tabasco

6 shots (150ml/6oz) Tio Pepe

1 strip lemon peel

1 sprig thyme

5 shakes (around half a gram) S&B nanami togarashi pepper

1 tsp black peppercorns

3g (¼oz) sliced fresh ginger

10g (0.4oz) sliced celery

1 tbsp fresh lemon juice

Just under 2 shots (40ml/1.6oz) vodka (ideally something spicy like Belvedere Rye, or something creamy like Chase)

Lemon, to garnish

I've served this around the world and have never failed to get the response that it's the best Bloody Mary ever (no pressure!). It's a drink that can get pretentiously overcomplicated (with lobster, cheeseburger and every condiment under the sun thrown in…), and while this version isn't simplistic, it's easy enough. Make the two main elements ahead of time, so you can be ready to go!

Method

Tomato mix (makes enough for about 6):
Dissolve the sweet white miso in 2 shots (50ml/2oz) hot water. Add the Worcestershire sauce, passata, tomato juice and Tabasco. Mix very well and keep covered.

Nuked sherry (makes enough for about 6):
Add the Tio Pepe to a microwave-safe container along with the lemon peel, thyme, nanami togarashi pepper, peppercorns, ginger and celery. Cover and blast in the microwave for 3 minutes. Allow to cool, then strain through a coffee filter.

To serve:
Fill a tall, straight-sided, narrow hi-ball with cubed ice, then add the lemon, just under 1 shot (20ml/0.8oz) nuked sherry, the vodka and 4 shots (100ml/4oz) tomato mix. Stir gently, top with more ice, and garnish with a slice of lemon.

TURKEY

I've worked in restaurants for much of my adult life, and holiday season tends to mean extra-long days – it makes having a day off to celebrate food with friends and family just that much sweeter. For the last ten-plus years, we have crammed into my little apartment in NYC for a potluck feast! We called it Tiensgiving. Everyone brings a dish that is special to them. I always make turkey and cornbread. We stuff our faces, drink and talk shop all night. These are still some of my best memories.

Since I don't have the space in my little kitchen to roast a whole turkey and all the sides, I break it down and fry the cutlets. It's a little extra work, but the result is really special. For the dressing, we make my wife Kate's grandmother's cornbread stuffing, and it's delicious! *Tien Ho*

Gather

Serves 6–8

12–16 boneless, skinless turkey breasts (2 per person)

Canola or rapeseed oil, to deep-fry

For the fish sauce vinaigrette

750ml (1⅓ pints/3 cups) fish sauce

500ml (18fl oz/2 cups) water

375g (13oz/2 cups) sugar

5 garlic cloves, finely chopped

Juice of 4 limes

125ml (4fl oz/½ cup) white wine vinegar

3 fresh Thai chillies, finely chopped

For the flour mix

500g (1lb 2oz/4 cups) plain (all-purpose) flour

3 tbsp bicarbonate of soda (baking soda)

1 tbsp salt

1 tbsp pepper

For the egg wash

3 eggs

125ml (4fl oz/½ cup) water

Method

Start preparing the turkey the day before you want to serve it. First, make the fish sauce vinaigrette by combining all the ingredients. Slice the turkey breasts into 1cm (½ inch) strips and leave to marinate in the vinaigrette for 24 hours.

When you are ready to cook (after the cornbread stuffing is in the oven, see p98), combine the ingredients for the flour mix and put in a shallow bowl. Mix the ingredients for the egg wash together well in a separate bowl.

Put the oil in a large pan, making sure it comes no higher than halfway up the pot. Heat to about 175°C (350°F). Remove the turkey from the marinade. Dredge the turkey first in flour, then egg wash and then flour again. Deep-fry a few turkey strips at a time until they are dark golden brown. Let them rest on a rack or on kitchen towels. Serve hot.

Serves 6–8

For Granny's cornbread

3 tbsp canola or rapeseed oil

250g (9oz/1½ cups) white fine cornmeal

1 tsp salt

1 tsp bicarbonate of soda (baking soda)

1 tsp caster (superfine) sugar

1 egg

500ml (18fl oz/2 cups) buttermilk

For the stuffing

8 celery sticks, chopped

1 large onion, chopped

225g (8oz/1 cup) butter

4 hotdog buns

8 eggs

8 large sage leaves

1–1½ litres (2–2½ pints/5–6 cups) chicken or turkey stock

Salt and pepper

GRANDMA MURRELL'S CORNBREAD STUFFING

Method

For the cornbread, preheat the oven to 230°C (450°F/gas mark 8). Pour the oil into a 23cm (9 inch) ovenproof cast-iron frying pan or similar heavy-based pan. Once the oven has heated up, put the pan in the oven to get piping hot.

Combine all the ingredients for the cornbread in a bowl and stir until well mixed. Pour the hot oil from the pan into the batter, then immediately pour the batter into the hot pan. Return to the oven and bake until brown on top and set – about 20 minutes. Remove from the oven and leave to cool.

When you are ready to make the stuffing, preheat the oven to 190°C (375°F/gas mark 5). Sauté the celery and onion with the butter, until tender and translucent.

Coarsely crumble the cornbread into a large bowl. Roughly tear the hot dog buns and mix with the cornbread. Add the sautéed vegetables to the breads. Stir in the eggs and sage, and season with salt and pepper. Stir in a small amount of warm turkey or chicken stock. My mom's instructions were to use enough stock to make it 'kind of soupy' – this doesn't mean like soup, but just so that the stuffing is wet enough that you can see a bit of stock come to the surface when it stands – in combination with the eggs, it will bind in the oven.

Pour the mix into a well-buttered pan or other baking dish. Dot the top with butter. Bake in the oven until very brown, set and puffy, about 1 hour. I like it to have very brown edges.

Gather

Serves 6

6 eggs

8 dashes orange blossom water

90g (3¼oz) demerara (light brown cane) sugar

6 shots (150ml/6oz) bourbon

2 shots (50ml/2oz) dark rum

2 shots (50ml/2oz) amaro

500ml (20oz) whole milk

1 vanilla pod

Salt

1 clove

Nutmeg, to garnish

TOM & JERRY

Bourbon, dark rum, orange blossom, amaro, egg, hot vanilla milk

Method

Separate the eggs. Whisk the whites with the orange blossom water. Whisk the yolks with the sugar, then whisk in the booze. Gently fold in the egg whites and keep the batter aside.

Heat the milk with the vanilla pod, a pinch of salt and the clove until hot, but not boiling, then fish out the spices.

Add just over two shots (60ml/2.4oz) batter to ceramic cups, then top with hot milk. Grate fresh nutmeg on top.

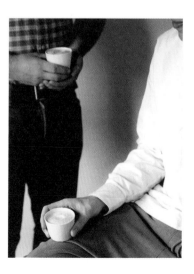

THANKS'A PUNCH

Applejack, sumac and grapefruit sherbet, hibiscus tea, champagne

With a lovely red colour and amazing acidity from the sumac, hibiscus, citrus and champagne, this punch is ideal alongside a hearty winter feast.

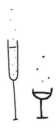

Gather

Makes 1 punch bowl

4 grapefruits

250g (9oz) white sugar

5g (1 tsp) sumac

15g (½oz) dried hibiscus

300ml (12oz) bonded applejack

1 bottle champagne

Method

Sumac and grapefruit sherbet:
Remove the zest of the grapefruits (ensuring no pith remains), and muddle with the sugar and sumac in a bowl. Allow to rest for at least 6 hours. Squeeze the juice from the grapefruits into the mix and stir well. When all the sugar is dissolved, pass through a sieve (but save some of the zests for garnish).

Hibiscus tea:
Add hibiscus flowers to a jug with 500ml (20oz) cold water. Allow to infuse for 6 hours in the fridge, then strain.

To serve:
Fill a punch bowl with a large block of ice, then add the sherbet and the tea, along with the bonded applejack, then top with the chilled bottle of champagne. Serve in chilled tea cups with ice.

Chet and Mark have created a dish that encourages putting effort into a very special dinner for friends. A little prep goes a long way, so I've dialled up the drink with similarly special twists to match the culinary showcase.

DINNER PARTY

with Mark Birchall & Chet Sharma, Restaurant Moor Hall

PLAICE COOKED IN TEA OIL

This is quite a restauranty dish, perfect for that intimate dinner where you want to impress. Don't panic, though, some elements can be skipped. Don't feel like an indulgent serving of mash? Boiled new potatoes could easily take their place. Similarly, the brined cabbage could happily be swapped out for some regular steamed greens.

However, I would encourage you to try the tea oil-cooked plaice. It's a fantastic flat fish that is readily available. Brining the fish first will firm up the flesh, so this is a key step.

Even the sous-vide cooking method can be missed out, but these water baths are becoming more common in homes and this is a great recipe to showcase the different uses for 'boil in a bag'. A carefully watched pan with a thermometer is a reasonable substitute, but won't give you the final product you see in top kitchens. *Mark Birchall & Chet Sharma*

Gather

Serves 4

For the tea oil

100g (3½oz) lapsang souchong loose-leaf tea

200ml (7fl oz/¾ cup) grapeseed oil

For the plaice

100g (3½oz/½ cup) sea salt

1 litre (1¾ pints/4 cups) water

4 x 150g (5½oz) boneless, skinless plaice fillets

For the brined cabbage

50g (1¾oz/¼ cup) salt

1 litre (1¾ pints/4 cups) water

1 sweetheart cabbage

Rapeseed oil, for frying

For the mash

1kg (2lb 4oz) Ratte potatoes

150ml (5fl oz/⅔ cup) whole milk

250g (9oz) salted organic butter

5g (1 tsp) salt (or to taste)

For the chicken jus

500ml (18fl oz/2 cups) fresh brown chicken stock

10ml (2 tsp) fresh lemon juice (about ¼ lemon)

Method

First, make the tea oil. Mix the lapsang souchong tea and grapeseed oil together in a sous-vide bag. Vacuum-seal and leave to infuse at 70°C (160°F) for 24 hours. Alternatively, bring the oil up to the same temperature in a pan, and add the tea, leaving to infuse off the heat overnight.

Remove the tea, strain the tea oil through a fine sieve and reserve in the fridge. This oil can be kept for at least 2 weeks.

Now prepare the plaice. Mix the salt and water together to make a brine, ensuring that all the salt has dissolved (this may require a little heat). Chill in the fridge. When the brine is cold, marinade the plaice fillets in it for 4 minutes. Remove from the brine and dry thoroughly.

Put the plaice fillets in separate sous-vide bags, with 50ml (2fl oz/⅓ cup) of the tea oil in each one, then vacuum-seal. Alternatively, add both to a shallow pan, ensuring that the whole fillets are covered with oil. Store in the fridge until required.

Now prepare the brined cabbage. Mix the salt and water together to make a brine. Quarter the sweetheart cabbage, removing any of the tough core. Place the cabbage quarters in separate sous-vide bags and add 250ml (9fl oz/1 cup) of the brine to each one. Vacuum-seal and leave for 30 minutes. Remove the cabbage from the bags and dry thoroughly on a kitchen cloth. Store in the fridge until required. If cooking without a sous-vide machine, simply grill the cabbage, then season.

Next, make the mash. Clean the potatoes of any dirt using a clean sponge. Place the potatoes in enough cold water to cover. Bring to the boil and cook until a knife can easily be inserted through a potato. Peel while hot, then run through a food mill or potato ricer.

Heat the milk in a separate pan until simmering and add to the riced potatoes. Mix the butter into the hot potato and milk mixture, being careful not to overwork. Season, then reserve in the refrigerator in a heatproof bag, such as a sous-vide or piping bag.

Finally, prepare the jus. Save yourself some work and buy in great-quality fresh chicken stock from the supermarket. Reduce the stock down to around 200ml (7fl oz/¾ cup). Reserve in the refrigerator.

When you are ready to serve, heat the mash up by placing the sealed bag in hot water. Remember, it is already cooked and only needs to be gently reheated.

Heat a large, heavy-bottomed frying pan over a medium–high heat. Add a little rapeseed oil and fry the brined cabbage until nicely caramelised on one side. Remove from the pan and keep warm in a low oven. Pop your plates in the oven to warm too.

Cook the plaice fillets for 6 minutes in a water bath set to 48°C (118°F). If cooking without a sous-vide machine, confit the fillets for the same amount of time in a pan of oil, being careful not to let the oil exceed 50°C (120°F).

Remove the fish from the bags or the pan and strain off any excess tea oil. To add a little colour, fry the fish in a very hot, dry frying pan for 20 seconds on the first side. Flip the fish and repeat on the other side. Remove from the pan, and leave to rest for a minute.

Meanwhile, pour the reduced stock into the frying pan to gain a little of the tea oil flavour and warm through. Add the lemon juice and remove from the heat.

Put a large spoonful of mash in the centre of a pre-warmed plate. Lay the plaice fillet at an angle across the plate, and balance the cabbage over the top. Drizzle with some of the tea oil and a spoonful of jus.

BUTTERED BUBBLES

Cachaça, burnt lemon, butter and bone-dry cava

'Fat washing' is a lovely way of getting big flavours into a drink without rich texture or weight. Here I've butter-washed some grassy Brazilian cachaça (it makes more than you need for one serve) to make it food-friendly – but this technique can be applied to lots of styles of spirit and drink.

Gather

75g (2 ½oz) unsalted butter

300ml (12oz) Yaguara Ouro cachaça

2 lemons

15g (½oz/1 tbsp) demerara (light brown cane) sugar

2 tsp acacia honey water (honey mixed 1:1 with warm water)

Recaredo Terrers cava, to top

1 string of redcurrants, to garnish

Method

Buttered cachaça:
Gently melt the unsalted butter, then pour into a narrow container with the aged cachaça, then mix. Transfer to the fridge and allow to cool. Skim the butter off the top, then strain the cachaça through a coffee filter.

Burnt lemon juice:
Top and tail the lemons, then cut along the equator. Lightly sprinkle with demerara sugar, then grill or blowtorch until lightly charred. When cooled, squeeze the lemons using a citrus press, and pass through a fine strainer.

To serve:
In a mixing glass, stir over ice: just over a shot (30ml/1.2oz) buttered Yaguara Ouro cachaça; a tablespoon of burnt lemon juice; and the honey water. Strain into a chilled cocktail glass and top with Recaredo Terrers cava, and garnish with a string of redcurrants.

CAKE &
COCKTAILS

with Signe Johansen,
'Scandilicious', 'How to Hygge'

A balanced cocktail is way better for an afternoon catch-up than a coffee! Signe's cake is light with a savoury note, but these cocktails also will work paired with richer, sweeter cakes and bakes.

CHERRY KIRSCH CAKE

In Scandinavia we never need an excuse for a slice of cake, and cherries give this one some real summertime zing. You can use raspberries, blueberries or a mix of forest fruits instead, but cherries work best with the cocktails. *Signe Johansen*

Gather

480g (17oz/2 cups) fresh pitted cherries (or use frozen, defrosted)

100ml (3½oz/scant ½ cup) kirsch liqueur, plus 2 tbsp for the cake mixture and a drizzle to serve

200g (7oz/scant 1 cup) lightly salted butter, at room temperature

150g (5½oz/¾ cup) golden caster (superfine) sugar

4 medium eggs

125g (4½oz/1 cup) plain, self-raising cake flour

200g (7oz/2⅓ cups) ground almonds

½ tsp baking powder

¼ tsp fine sea salt

1 tbsp plain yogurt

Toasted almond flakes, to decorate

Method

Preheat the oven to 170°C (325°F/gas mark 3). Lightly grease and line a 23cm (9 inch) round baking tin (with a detachable bottom) with baking paper.

In a medium bowl, soak the cherries in the kirsch liqueur.

In a large mixing bowl, beat the butter and sugar until pale and creamy (about 10 minutes).

Add each egg, one at a time, with a spoonful of flour to prevent the mixture from splitting. Beat well, so each egg incorporates with the butter mixture.

Add the rest of the ingredients, including the 2 tablespoons of kirsch, and gently fold everything together so you don't knock out the air added while creaming the butter.

Place the tipsy cherries and their liqueur at the bottom of the lined cake tin, making sure they're in an even layer.

Carefully dollop the cake mixture over the cherries and use the back of the spoon or spatula to smooth the mixture so it's even.

Bake in the middle of the oven for 1 hour. If you have a fan oven, check after 40 minutes – the cake should look golden brown on top and feel firm to the touch. If in doubt, insert a skewer and it should come out with no raw mixture on it. If you have an older oven or one that's a little temperamental, it may take a little longer to bake this cake. Be patient and keep an eye on it.

Remove the cake from the oven and cool on a wire rack. Once cooled, tip it out upside down on a platter or board and gently remove the baking paper.

You can add an extra drizzle of kirsch liqueur over the cherry topping if you wish!

Serve as is, or scatter over some toasted almond flakes to decorate.

REVERSE CHERRY GIBSON

Gin, vermouth and corpse reviver cherries

This 'reverse' martini weights the gin and vermouth ratio in favour of the vermouth for a lighter serve. This is contrasted with some sweet acidity from the pickled cherry. The brands here make good partners, but experiment away!

Gather

Half vanilla pod

4 shots (100ml/4oz) cider vinegar

50g (1¾oz) sugar

3 strips orange peel

1 stick cinnamon

100g (3½oz) fresh cherries (Rainier if possible)

Just under 1 shot (20ml/0.8oz) absinthe

4 shots (200ml/4oz) Cointreau

Just under 2 shots (40ml/1.6oz) Martini Extra Dry vermouth

1 tbsp Star of Bombay gin

Method

Pickled cherries:
Scrape out the vanilla seeds and put them and the pod in a pan with the cider vinegar, sugar, orange peel and cinnamon. Heat over a medium heat for 10 minutes then allow to cool. Add to a clean preserving jar with fresh cherries, absinthe and Cointreau. Leave to infuse in the fridge for at least 2 weeks.

To serve:
Stir vermouth and gin over ice. Strain into a frozen cocktail glass and garnish with a pickled cherry.

CUPBOARD COCKTAIL

White tea, raspberry and salt

This uses things that are stable and always in the house (they are in mine at least!) and can be twisted with different teas and jams, but like a cake, it can always be rustled up. It's boozeless, but takes a spike of gin if need be!

Gather

7g (⅓oz) white tea

1 tsp raspberry jam

Pinch sea salt

Method

Brew white tea in 8 shots (200ml/8oz) water at 85°C/185°F water for 4 minutes and allow to cool. Put 6 shots (150ml/6oz) in a cocktail shaker then throw with the jam and salt – to do this, fill one side of the shaker with ice, then using a strainer, 'throw' the liquid in a long arc and catch in the empty tin, repeat – pouring the liquid over ice each time. Then strain into a small hi-ball or rocks glass filled with ice.

CAKE OR DEATH

Coffee, cassis, aquavit and vanilla cream

This is my update on the Irish coffee – and it's distinctly not Irish! Whiskey matches the dark, burnt-toffee notes of cheap coffee (which is, of course, fine to use). But I find herbal, red berry brightness when using good coffee.

Gather

10g (⅓oz) freshly ground coffee

4 shots (100ml/4oz) double (heavy) cream

1 vanilla pod

Sugar (if required)

1 shot (25ml/1oz) aquavit

Just under 1 shot (20ml/0.8oz) crème de cassis

Method

Brew the coffee with 6 shots (150ml/6oz) boiling water. Filter and keep warm.

Gently whip double cream with the seeds of the vanilla pod, and a little sugar if desired.

Fill a hot-temperature-safe glass (a thick-walled hi-ball or a stemmed glass) with hot water, then discard. Add the booze, top with hot coffee, then spoon over vanilla cream.

I'm lucky to work with some of the best folk in the world, so it made sense to ask them for some drinks that really suit big groups. I'm in charge of the food for this one, and I've kept it light and easy to eat with your fingers.

WATCHING
THE GAME

with Mr Lyan, White Lyan (RIp), Dandelyan and
all them other things

Makes 1 bottle

20g (¾oz) mint

20g (¾oz) tarragon

200g (7oz) sugar

300ml (12oz) rye genever

8 shots (200ml/8oz) mineral water

2 shots (50ml/2oz) lime cordial

3 shots (75ml/3oz) oaked Chardonnay

Champagne, to top

Extra mint sprigs, to garnish

GENIE IN A BOTTLE BY ROBIN HONHOLD

Rye genever, mint & tarragon syrup, lime cordial, oaked Chardonnay and bubbles!

Method

Mint & tarragon syrup:
Blanch the mint and tarragon (including stems) by submerging in boiling water for 15 seconds then plunging into iced water to refresh. Add drained herbs to a blender with the sugar and 8 shots (200ml/8oz) cold water and blitz until very cold and very green, then strain through a cheesecloth. (This makes more syrup than you need here but it's also awesome drunk with soda!)

Bottle up all the ingredients (apart from the extra mint and champagne) with 5 shots (125ml/4½oz) mint & tarragon syrup. Mix and keep chilled.

To serve:
Add 3 shots (75ml/3oz) to a chilled flute, then top with an equal amount of champagne. Garnish with a sprig of mint.

PEACH & FINO COBBLER
BY AIDAN BOWIE

Fino, peach jam, lemon and grapefruit soda

Gather

2 shots (50ml/2oz) fino sherry

Just under 1 shot (20ml/0.8oz)
lemon juice

2 tsp peach jam

1 pinch salt

Grapefruit soda, to top

Garden herbs, to garnish

Method

Add to a shaker the fino, lemon, jam
and salt. Short shake with ice, strain
into a rocks glass with ice, then top
with grapefruit soda. Garnish with
green herbs.

For the fish mix

3g (1½ tsp) freshly ground black pepper

1g (½ tsp) cumin seeds

1g (½ tsp) mild curry powder

1g (½ tsp) coriander seeds

1 clove

Seeds from 1 cardamom pod

20ml (1½ tbsp) olive oil

7g (2 tsp) finely chopped garlic cloves
(about 2 cloves)

5g (1 tsp) finely chopped ginger

75g (2½oz/⅓ cup) finely
chopped red onion

2 curry leaves

2 x 120g (4oz) tins of tuna, drained

30g (1oz/2 tbsp) tinned anchovies in
oil, drained

15ml (1 tbsp) fresh lime juice
(about ½ lime)

For the croquetas

60g (2¼oz/¼ cup) unsalted butter

60g (2¼oz/½ cup) plain (all-purpose)
flour, plus extra for dusting

500ml (18fl oz/2 cups) hot, not boiled,
full-fat milk

2 organic eggs

200g (7oz/2¼ cups) panko
breadcrumbs

Vegetable oil or similar neutral oil,
for deep-frying

Nutmeg, to serve

CUTLET CROQUETAS

This is my mash-up of Mama Chet's Sri Lankan fish cutlets and the super-moreish Spanish croquetas. These are fabulous to feed to guests when they first arrive. They're best freshly cooked, but can be kept warm in the oven as people turn up, so they're ready for snacking on with the welcome drinks.

Ryan Chetiyawardana

Method

First, dry-roast all the spices for the fish mix individually in a dry frying pan over a low heat until fragrant. Leave to cool, combine and grind into a fine powder.

Heat the oil in a large saucepan over a medium heat, and gently sauté the spice mix, garlic, ginger, onion and curry leaves for about 5 minutes until soft but not coloured. Add the tuna and the anchovies, sauté for a further 5–10 minutes, then add the lime juice and stir. Set aside to cool.

Next, make a golden roux with the butter and flour in a pan. Gradually add the hot milk, stirring constantly. Mix in the fish mixture. Keep on a medium-low heat, stirring constantly until you get a stiff mixture (kind of like mashed potatoes). Transfer to a bowl and refrigerate for 2 hours.

When you are ready to make the croquetas, beat the eggs in a shallow bowl, and spread the breadcrumbs in a separate shallow dish.

Flour your hands and take out scoops of the mixture and shape into small oval croquetas, about 4cm x 2cm (1½ x ¾ inch). Set on a floured surface until the mixture is all portioned out. Roll in egg, then in breadcrumbs. Repeat until all the croquetas are coated.

Heat a pan of oil to 180°C (350°F) and fry in small batches until golden. Remove and lay on kitchen towel to absorb the excess oil and grate nutmeg over the top. Serve as they're cooked for the troops to pick at.

ATOMIC BELLE BY MAJA JAWORSKA

Tequila, lemon, smoked salt, basil, grapefruit & plum shrub

Method

For the shrub, add all to a microwave-safe container (except the lemon and tequila) and blast for 5 minutes (or cook on medium heat in a pan for 10 minutes). Allow to cool, then strain.

Fill a hi-ball with ice and add the tequila, lemon juice and 3 shots (75ml/3oz) shrub and two torn basil leaves. Garnish with a slice of plum.

Gather

3 strips grapefruit peel

5 large sweet basil leaves

2 large red plums, sliced (200g/7oz)

2 tsp smoked sea salt

130g (4½oz) white sugar

65ml (2¼oz) cider vinegar

445ml (15½oz) water

A shot-and-a-half (35ml/1.4oz) tequila

Just under 1 shot (20ml/0.8oz) lemon juice

Extra basil and plum, to serve

124

1 tsp honey

1 tbsp lemon juice

1 shot (25ml/1oz) of your
favourite whisk(e)y

6 shots (150ml/6oz) white beer

Blood orange, to garnish

HALF 'N' HALF TODDY BY ALLY KELSEY

Honey, lemon, whisk(e)y and weiss beer

Method

Add lemon, honey and whisk(e)y to a
hi-ball and stir to dissolve. Fill with ice.
Top with beer and stir. Garnish with a
wedge of blood (or regular) orange.

SEAWITCH SPRITZ
BY KELSEY RAMAGE

Riesling, cranberry, thyme, crème de mure and soda

Gather

1 bottle dry Riesling

20 cranberries

Peel of 5 grapefruits

3 sprigs thyme (plus 1 to garnish)

2 tsp agave

2 tsp crème de mure

Soda, to top

Method

Infuse the wine with the smashed cranberries, grapefruit peel and thyme overnight, then strain.

Mix the agave and liqueur with 4 shots (100ml/4oz) infused wine over ice in a wine glass or tumbler, stir then top with soda. Garnish with a sprig of thyme.

75g (2½oz/⅓ cup) raw or cultured butter

1 medium cauliflower, leaves left on

30ml (2 tbsp) raw cider vinegar

15g (½oz) dried Maldive fish

3g (1½ tsp) yellow mustard seeds

Salt and pepper

Parsley, chopped, to garnish

POT-ROAST CAULIFLOWER WITH CULTURED BUTTER AND MALDIVE FISH

This is very easy to prepare for a group. It works well with a whole red cabbage too, but I love the creaminess of cauliflower with the chicken (see p135). The acidity of the cultured butter cuts through the richness, but regular unsalted butter and cider vinegar is just fine too. Dried Maldive fish can be bought from Asian supermarkets, and add depth, but it can be omitted if you want to keep it veggie friendly. *RC*

Method

Preheat the oven to 180°C (350°F/gas mark 4). Heat a large ovenproof pan (with a lid) on the hob over a medium heat. Add the butter, then the cauliflower, florets down, and cook for 5 minutes. Turn over, add the cider vinegar, Maldive fish, mustard seeds and seasoning, and cover. Place in the oven and roast for 30 minutes. Remove from the oven, lift on to a serving dish, drizzle the pan liquor over the top, then scatter with chopped parsley and serve with a big-ass knife.

SMOKED NACIONAL PUNCH
BY IAIN GRIFFITHS

Golden rum, apricot brandy, lemon sherbet,
lapsang souchong tea and Worcestershire sauce

Method

Lemon sherbet:
Infuse the zest of 6 lemons with the sugar overnight or in a vac-pack bag. Hydrate with the juice from the six lemons and mix well.

To serve:
Add to a punch bowl the sherbet, rum, liqueur, lemon juice, tea and Worcestershire sauce. Stir over a block of ice, then serve in rocks glasses filled with ice.

Gather

Makes 1 punch bowl

6 lemons

480g (17oz) sugar

350ml (14oz) golden rum

7 shots (175ml /7oz) apricot liqueur

6 shots (150ml/6oz) lemon juice

500ml (20oz) strong, cold lapsang souchong tea

1 tsp Worcestershire sauce

Gather

1½kg (3lb 5oz) organic chicken legs (6 pieces)

Vegetable oil or other neutral oil, for frying

1 bunch breakfast or rainbow radishes, to serve

For the buttermilk brine

500ml (18fl oz/2 cups) buttermilk

2 tsp smoked paprika

2 garlic cloves, sliced

2 fresh rosemary sprigs

1 fresh parsley sprig (just the stalks work well too, so save them if you've used the leaves elsewhere)

1 thyme sprig (stalk only, use the leaves in the coating)

Salt and pepper

For the coating flour

200g (7oz/1½ cups) plain (all-purpose) flour

3g (1⅓ tbsp) fresh thyme leaves

3g (½ tsp) celery salt

2g (½ tsp) cracked pepper

10g (1⅓ tbsp) onion powder

For the Bloody Mary butter

300ml (½ pint/1¼ cups) whipping or double (heavy) cream

1 tbsp Worcestershire sauce

½ tsp Tabasco

1 tsp tomato paste

Salt and pepper

FRIED CHICKEN WITH RADISHES AND BLOODY MARY BUTTER

This is a simple but crowd-pleasing recipe, to satisfy the craving for fried chicken! It's pretty rich, so it's amazing with the roasted cauliflower, but I also like serving some green cabbage sautéed with tarragon and hazelnut to balance it. Some simple warm bread, or ideally some *pao de queijo*, is a fine accompaniment too. The whipped butter is perfect with both the chicken and the mustard bite of the breakfast radishes. Add more spice if you're not a wuss like me. *RC*

Method

Mix all the ingredients for the buttermilk brine together and coat the chicken well. Marinate for 12 hours sealed up or covered in the fridge.

Mix the coating flour ingredients together (and add any leftover panko breadcrumbs from the croquetas) and put in a shallow bowl.

Remove the chicken pieces from the marinade and coat in the flour. Set aside. Preheat the oven to 180°C (350°F/gas mark 4), unless it's already on for the cauliflower.

Heat the oil in a shallow pan over a medium heat and, in batches of two, seal the chicken pieces until golden on both sides. Transfer to a roasting pan and finish in the oven for 15 minutes or until cooked through, and the juices run clear.

To make the Bloody Mary butter, add all the ingredients to an electric mixer, and beat until light and fluffy.

Serve the fried chicken with radishes and a side of the whipped butter.

AN INDIAN EXTRAVAGANZA

with Karan Gokani, Hoppers

This is the sort of meal that balances the finesse of fine dining with a dinner that comforts, and doesn't seem showy to your friends. You can spend time with them, rather than be locked away in the kitchen, but the flavours are incredible. An amazing meal for spice aficionados and newbies alike! The drinks have a touch of the exotic to them, but are rooted in classic serves.

SINGHA SOUR

Arrack, aquavit, cucumber, cumin, lavender and lemon

Gather

1 slice cucumber (plus a strip to garnish)

8 cumin seeds

Pinch salt

1 shot (25ml/1oz) Ceylon arrack

1 shot (25ml/1oz) Linie aquavit

Just under 1 shot (20ml/0.8oz) lemon juice

1 tbsp lavender syrup

1 dash Peychaud's bitters

Method

Muddle the cucumber in the bottom of a shaker with the cumin seeds and salt. Add the other ingredients. Shake hard, and double strain into a chilled cocktail glass. Garnish with a strip of cucumber.

COCONUT RAMOS

Colombo gin, coconut, rice, kewra, egg white, lemon, soda, candied ginger

Gather

Syphon serves 6

250ml (10oz) Colombo gin

120ml (4.8oz) lemon juice

6 shots (150ml/6oz) rice milk

90ml (3¾oz) Coco López coconut cream

120ml (4.8oz) egg white

6 shots (150ml/6oz) water

2 shots (50ml/2oz) sugar syrup

2 dashes orange blossom

1 dash kewra water

6 cubes candied ginger, to garnish

Method

Whisk all ingredients apart from the ginger then add to a soda syphon and chill well. Charge with one bulb of nitrogen and one of carbon dioxide.

Carefully dispense into flutes, then garnish with a cube of candied ginger.

Indian food is ideal for a feast with friends. At home, we often serve up a first course that's individually plated and then invite guests into the kitchen to help themselves to the main, which is laid out on our breakfast bar. The plated starter is an impressive way to begin a meal and can buy you some time to reheat the mains. *Karan Gokani*

PATRA NI MACCHI (FISH WRAPPED IN BANANA LEAF)

This Parsi dish has a very special place in my heart. In Bombay, where I grew up, we use whole pomfret for this dish, but I find sea bass or rainbow trout work very well too. I have written this recipe as a starter, and therefore use fillets. If you prefer to serve it as a main or a shared starter, use a whole fish instead. You'll just need a little more chutney and 5–8 minutes longer in the steamer. *KG*

Gather

Serves 4 as a starter

½ tsp salt

½ tsp ground turmeric

Juice of half a lime

4 seabass fillets (approx 150–200g (5½–7oz) each)

2 large banana leaves

4 wooden cocktail sticks or toothpicks, soaked in water

For the chutney

¾ bunch fresh coriander (cilantro), leaves and tender stalks only

½ bunch of fresh mint, leaves only

3 garlic cloves

1cm (½ inch) fresh ginger

1 tbsp roasted peanuts

½ tsp cumin seeds, gently roasted

½ tsp granulated sugar

1 fresh green chilli (or less if you want it milder)

Juice of half a lime (or more if you like)

¾ tsp salt, or more to taste

Method

Mix the salt, turmeric and lime juice together, and marinate the fish in it for 30–60 minutes.

Blitz all the ingredients for the chutney in a blender to a smooth paste.

Carefully pass the banana leaves over a flame or pour boiling water over them to make them supple and prevent them from splitting when folded. Cut off the thick ribs and trim each leaf into two rectangles.

Place each fillet in the middle of a banana leaf and coat generously with the chutney. Then wrap the leaf around the fish tightly and secure with a cocktail stick. (You can prepare the parcels on the morning of the party and leave them in the fridge until ready to cook. Add a couple of minutes to the steaming time if cooking from chilled.)

Steam the parcels in a bamboo steamer or other steamer for 10 minutes. (If you don't have a steamer, you can double-wrap the parcels in baking paper and foil, and pop them in a baking tray with ½ cup of water and a splash of vinegar. Bake in the oven at 160°C (325°F/gas mark 3), for 14 minutes.)

Serve the steaming parcels in the leaves so your guests can unwrap them on the table. This adds an element of drama and the aromas come wafting out of the parcels as they are opened.

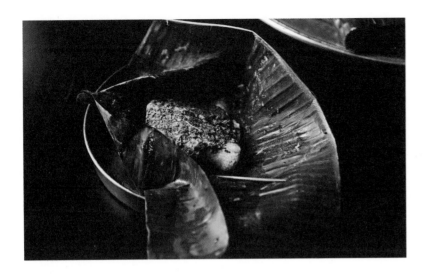

CURRY LEAF RAITA

This is adapted from my wife's mum's raita recipe. It's probably one of the first dishes I ate at their house, and still one of my favourite accompaniments to a curry or biryani. *KG*

Gather

Serves 4 as a side

400g (14oz/1⅔ cups) thick Greek yogurt

2 tsp rapeseed or vegetable oil

½ tsp mustard seeds

1 fresh green chilli, finely chopped (optional)

1cm (½ inch) ginger, finely chopped

⅓ tsp ground turmeric

8–10 fresh curry leaves

Salt, to taste

Method

Season the yogurt to taste and pop in the fridge to chill.

Heat the oil in the smallest frying pan you have, set on a medium heat. Once the oil is hot, add the mustard seeds. These should gently splutter as soon as they are added to the oil – if they don't, the oil is not hot enough. Add one seed at a time to test this.

Once the spluttering dies down a little, add the chilli, ginger, turmeric and curry leaves, and remove the heat immediately. Let these heat through for a minute, then ripple the beautiful golden oil through the chilled yogurt. Don't mix the oil into the yogurt completely, as the marbled/rippled effect looks stunning and eliminates the need for a garnish. Serve immediately.

Note

This tempered or spiced oil is called a 'tarka' in India. You can prepare the tarka ahead of time and leave it in the pan. This can be warmed through and added to the yogurt when you are ready to serve.

TARKA DAL CHAAT (SPICED LENTILS WITH AN ARRAY OF CONDIMENTS)

Lentils are known as 'dal' in India and are a mealtime staple. The most common lentil dish is similar to a soup and eaten with rice at the end of a meal. When we entertain at home, we enjoy making our dishes interactive so people can get involved and customise them to their liking. So we often make the simple tarka dal a bit more exciting by adding an array of toppings/condiments to it. *KG*

Gather

Serves 4 as a generous side

For the dal

200g (7oz/1 cup) split and husked green mung beans (moong dal). This dish can also be made with split red lentils (masoor dal)

1 tbsp rapeseed or vegetable oil

1 medium onion, finely chopped

1½ tsp salt, or more to taste

2 cloves

600ml–1 litre (20fl oz/2½ cups–34fl oz/4 cups) water or light vegetable stock (traditionally, dals aren't cooked in stock, but I find using a light vegetable stock or a mix of water and stock gives this dish greater depth)

1 tsp ground turmeric

1½ tsp garam masala (see p147)

For the tempering

2 tbsp ghee (or unsalted butter)

5 garlic cloves, sliced

1 tsp cumin seeds

1½ tsp chilli powder

Optional condiments

Finely chopped fresh coriander (cilantro)

Finely chopped fresh green chillies

Finely sliced fresh tomatoes, seeds removed

Fried shallots (you can fry these yourself or buy them in jars at most Asian supermarkets)

Crushed roasted peanuts

Indian chaat masala (you can find this wonderfully tangy spice mix at most Indian supermarkets; or use a lightly roasted garam masala)

Lime wedges

Method

Wash the lentils thoroughly in cold water till the water runs clear (about 8–10 times). Once washed, leave to soak in water for 30 minutes to 2 hours.

Heat 2 teaspoons of the oil in a pan and add the chopped onion, cloves and salt. Cook on a medium heat until the onion is golden brown. Add the washed lentils, water or stock and the turmeric and simmer uncovered for 20–30 minutes, or until the lentils are very soft and most of the water has been absorbed. Add more boiling water and continue to cook if the lentils aren't soft enough. Adjust salt to your taste and add boiling water if you prefer a thinner dal.

Dry-roast the garam masala in a dry pan over a low heat until very fragrant then stir it into the dal. Simmer for 2 more minutes and take off the heat.

In a small pan, add the ghee or butter for the tempering and heat till it melts. Add the garlic and cook on a low heat till it sizzles and goes golden. Add the cumin seeds, and when they begin to crackle add the chilli powder. Cook for 30 seconds on a very low heat. Do not allow the chilli powder to burn or turn black. Take it off the heat immediately if it begins to get dark.

Pour this spiced butter over the dal and sprinkle with the chopped coriander, if using. Serve immediately.

LAMB SHANK BERRY BIRYANI

Very few dishes lend themselves to a feast like a gorgeous pilau or a biryani. Both these terms are names for aromatic rice and meat/vegetable dishes, and are often used interchangeably. Technically speaking, though, they are prepared in different ways. For a pilau, the rice and meat are usually sautéed together and then cooked in a measured quantity of water. Sometimes the rice and meat are even cooked separately then pan-fried together. For a biryani the marinated meat is layered with par-cooked rice and cooked together in a sealed pot. The rice is effectively cooked in the steam from the meat. In this recipe, I take a famous pilau and make it using the biryani technique. *KG*

Gather

Serves 4

1½kg (3lb 5oz) lamb shank on the bone, each shank cut into 2 or 3 pieces

4 tbsp ghee or unsalted butter

2 tbsp fried onions

1 tbsp chopped coriander (cilantro)

For the spice mix

4 black cardamom pods

6–8 green cardamom pods

6–8 cloves

7½cm (3 inches) cinnamon or cassia bark

2 bay leaves

1 tsp ground black pepper

1½ tsp cumin seeds

2 tsp coriander seeds, crushed

For the marinade

2 tbsp rapeseed or vegetable oil

5cm (2 inches) ginger, roughly chopped

4 garlic cloves, roughly chopped

300g (10½oz/1¼ cup) thick Greek yogurt

4 tbsp golden fried onions

2 tbsp Kashmiri red chilli powder

½ tsp ground turmeric

2 tsp tomato purée (paste), double concentrate

2 tbsp fresh coriander (cilantro), chopped

2 tsp salt, or more to taste

For the rice

2 black cardamom pods

3 green cardamom pods

4 cloves

2 bay leaves

3 tbsp salt, or more to taste

450g (1lb/2 cups) long-grain basmati rice (the best quality you can find)

For the garnish

2 tbsp cashew nuts, fried in ghee

3 tbsp dried barberries, soaked in water overnight (or 1½ tbsp dried cranberries or raisins), then fried in a tablespoon of butter for 30 seconds to preserve the red colour

2 tbsp fresh coriander (cilantro), chopped

A generous pinch of saffron strands, crushed with a pestle and mortar and soaked in 1 tbsp warm milk (optional)

Note

Seasoning and timing are crucial to a successful biryani and you will need to practise this recipe a few times and tweak the cooking times and amount of salt used to make it work for you. The thickness and size of the pan you use, the amount of water you boil your rice in, and the quality of rice used will all have an impact on the timing and seasoning.

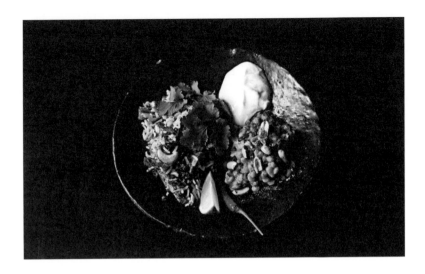

Method

Dry-roast each spice for the spice mix separately in a heavy-based pan set over a low heat, until it releases its aromas. (Leave the cardamom seeds in their pods to roast.) Mix the spices and allow them to cool completely. Once cooled, grind them to a very fine powder in a spice grinder. (You can make a large batch of the spice mix and keep it stored in an airtight jar for up to a month in a cool, dark cupboard. This can be substituted for garam masala in other recipes.)

Add the oil, ginger and garlic from the marinade ingredients to the powder and continue to blitz until you have a fine paste. Add a splash of water if required.

Transfer the spice paste to a large mixing bowl and add all the other ingredients for the marinade and mix well. The marinade should be slightly saltier than you like because this will be seasoning the lamb.

Add the lamb shank pieces to the mixing bowl and massage the marinade into them thoroughly. Cover and chill in the fridge for at least 6 hours or preferably overnight.

When ready to cook the biryani, wash the rice thoroughly in cold water until the water runs clear. Then leave the rice to soak for 30 minutes, submerged in cold water.

Bring a large pan of water to the boil. Add the spices and salt for the rice to the water and when it comes to the boil, add the drained rice.

At the same time, melt 2 tablespoons of the ghee or butter in a cast-iron casserole pan or similar heavy-based pan with a tightly fitting lid, on a medium heat, and add the marinated meat. Stir the meat a couple of times, sprinkle the fried onions and chopped coriander over the top, and bring the heat down to just above the minimum.

Once the rice has cooked for 4–5 minutes and seems half-cooked, use a slotted spoon to transfer it into the other pan, on top of the meat, straining as much water as possible out each time. (To check if it is half-cooked, press a grain with your fingers and make sure the outer layer is soft but the inside is still firm and holds its shape.)

Once all the rice has been transferred over to the meat pan, sprinkle all the ingredients for the garnish over the top, dot the remaining 2 tablespoons of the ghee or butter over the rice and seal tightly. If the lid does not close completely, cover the pot with a layer of baking paper, two layers of foil and the lid. It is essential that the lid tightly seals the pot you use to make the biryani, keeping the steam in (known as 'dum'). Cooks in India often seal the pot with dough to ensure it is completely airtight.

Cook on a low heat undisturbed for 1 hour. Serve immediately or keep covered and warm in an oven set to 30°C (90°F/lowest possible gas mark) for up to 2 hours.

This dish is best served in the pan, lifting the lid just before eating, so all the wonderful aromas are kept in the pot.

PASSIONFRUIT AND MANGO PAVLOVA

This is a simple yet gorgeous take on a pavlova. Mangoes and passionfruit are a wonderful match, while the dense mascarpone cream provides a lovely contrast to the airy meringue. *KG*

Notes

This is a very simple dessert that you can prepare ahead of a party. Once cooled, keep the meringue wrapped in cling film or in an airtight box, and only top with cream just before serving.

You can make individual meringues if you prefer to serve individual portions. The baking time should be reduced to 45 minutes or a little less, depending on their size. Once cooked through the meringue should peel off the baking paper easily.

Gather

Serves 4

For the meringue

5 egg whites

½ tsp salt

1 tsp vanilla extract

250g (9oz/1⅓ cup) granulated sugar

For the topping

150g (5½oz/⅔ cup) mascarpone cheese

125ml (4fl oz/½ cup) double (heavy) cream

2 tbsp icing sugar (powdered sugar)

90g (3¼oz/⅓ cup) fresh or tinned mango pulp

2 fresh ripe passionfruits

1 fresh mint sprig, leaves only

Method

Preheat the oven to 140°C (275°F/gas mark 1).

In a completely dry bowl, whisk the egg whites and salt on a medium speed, until the whites form stiff peaks and you can turn the bowl upside down without it all falling out.

Add the vanilla extract and a third of the sugar and continue to whisk on high speed for about 15–20 seconds. The whites will begin to look glossy now. Add another third of the sugar and whisk away for a further 15–20 seconds. Finally, add the remaining sugar and whisk on low for 15–20 seconds or until the whites hold their shape when the whisk is taken out. Resist the temptation to over-whisk the eggs at each stage. The eggs will tend to split if over-whisked and the result will be a dense, super-sweet biscuit instead of a light airy meringue. The ideal consistency should be similar to a glossy shaving foam.

Spoon the meringue mix on to a silicone baking sheet or oven tray lined with baking paper in a large circle, and run swirls around the edges with a spatula or skewer.

Put in the oven and bake for 70 minutes without opening the door. Turn the oven off, but don't open the door. Leave for another 15 minutes, then remove the meringue and cool on a wire rack.

Once cooled, peel off the baking paper and place on your serving plate.

Lightly whisk together the mascarpone, double cream and icing sugar in a mixing bowl until well mixed and quite light and airy. Roughly spoon this over the meringue and drizzle the mango and passionfruit pulp over the cream. You can also scatter the mint leaves on top if you like. Serve immediately.

FINGERROOT DRY DAIQUIRI

White rum, Ceylon tea, lemon, lime, passionfruit pulp, Campari

Gather

1 tsp loose-leaf Ceylon black tea

8 shots (200ml/8oz) white rum

2 tsp lime juice

1 tsp lemon juice

Pulp of half a passionfruit

1 tsp Campari

2 tsp sugar syrup

1 stem fingerroot ginger, to garnish

Method

Tea-infused rum (makes enough for 4 or so serves):
Infuse the tea in the rum for 5 minutes, then strain. This is quite a strong infusion without being too bitter. You can use the leaves again for a fruitier second infusion though. Use the good stuff!

To serve:
Add to a shaker just under 2 shots (40ml/1.6oz) tea-infused white rum, the lime and lemon juices, the passionfruit pulp, the Campari and the sugar. Shake hard, then double strain into a small chilled glass. Garnish with a split stem of fingerroot ginger rubbed around the lip of the glass and dropped in.

It's true, this recipe requires a good bit of effort. But trust me, if there's one night you should be putting in a bit of effort, it's date night!

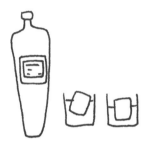

DATE NIGHT

with Joan Roca, El Celler de Can Roca

RARE CASK OLD FASHIONED

The Macallan Rare Cask, demerara, bitter cacao,
dark roasted coffee, clove and fried orange

The dessert on the following page is a serious dish to make for someone you're, erm, serious about, and fittingly this is one serious cocktail! The Macallan Rare Cask is proper splash-out whisky, and the cocktail is carefully nuanced to be sensitive to that – don't be scared of using your most precious ingredients in this way if it's for the right setting, especially if your drink is made with care and attention. (In other words, this might not be one for a 2am post-party cocktail.)

Gather

100g (3½oz) demerara (light brown cane) sugar

1 pounded raw cacao bean

3 cracked coffee beans (the dark glossy ones that make terrible coffee, but are useful for bitterness!)

1 clove

1 pinch of salt

Just over 2 shots (60ml/2.4oz) The Macallan Rare Cask

1 orange

Method

Put sugar, cacao bean, coffee beans, clove and pinch of salt in a pre-warmed bowl and add 3 shots (75ml/3oz) boiling water. Whisk until the sugar and salt are dissolved, then pass through a fine sieve.

Meanwhile, slice the orange into rounds, and gently sear in a pan to give a little colour on each side and caramelise some of the sugars. Pat dry, allow to cool, then transfer to the fridge.

Stir 2 teaspoons infused sugar in a mixing glass with the whisky. Pour over a large cube of ice, and garnish with a slice of grilled orange.

CIGAR BOX

Serves 1

WHISKY PARFAIT

Gather

200ml (7fl oz/¾ cup) The Macallan Amber

800ml (1½ pints/3⅓ cups) double (heavy) cream

100g (3½oz) egg yolks (about 5)

50g (1¾oz/¼ cup) caster (superfine) sugar

400g (14oz) 40% chocolate (preferably Rocolat by Cacao Barry), chopped

Method

Reduce the whisky by half in a saucepan on a low flame, until you have 100ml (3½fl oz/scant ½ cup). Set aside.

Gently simmer the cream in a small pan. Mix the egg yolks and the sugar, and add to the cream to make a custard. Warm through, whisking continuously, until it is 82°C (180°F). Add the chopped chocolate, melt and homogenise the mixture. Add the still lukewarm whisky reduction and set aside while you make the meringue.

SWISS MERINGUE

Gather

8 sheets leaf gelatine

300g (10½oz) egg whites (about 8)

200g (7oz/1 cup) caster (superfine) sugar

Method

Soak the gelatine sheets in a bowl with a few tablespoons of water and plenty of ice.

In a water bath, mix the egg white with the sugar until it is 60°C (140°F), while continuously stirring with the help of a few rods. Take the sheets of gelatine out of the water and dry them well. Put them in a bowl, together with the egg white mixture. Place the bowl under the electric blender, and blend until it is completely cold.

Line a flat tray, 2cm (¾ inch) tall, with wrinkled baking paper so that the cigar box will look like wood. Spread the parfait mixture out on the tray, then add the Swiss meringue, making circling movements with a spatula. Leave to set for 24 hours.

PLUM AND TOBACCO PURÉE

Gather

1 cigar

6 litres (1½ gallons) water

2kg (4lb 8oz) pitted plums

Method

Put the cigar in a pan with 2 litres (3½ pints/8 cups) of cold water. Bring to the boil and when it reaches boiling point, carefully remove the cigar and empty the water.

Repeat this process twice more with the remaining water. On the last boil, remove the cigar but preserve the blanching water.

Put the water in a food processor along with the pitted plums. Mix, strain through a fine sieve and set aside.

WHISKY AND CIGAR WATER GELATINE

CRYSTALLISED CIGAR LEAF

Gather

1 cigar

6 litres (1½ gallons) water

6g (⅛oz) kappa (gelling agent extracted from seaweed)

120g (4¼oz/½ cup) caster (superfine) sugar

300ml (10fl oz/1¼ cups) The Macallan Amber

Method

Put the cigar in a pan with 2 litres (3½ pints/8 cups) of cold water. Bring to the boil and when it reaches boiling point, carefully remove the cigar and empty the water. Repeat this process twice more with the remaining water. On the last boil, remove the cigar but preserve the blanching water.

Measure 300ml (10fl oz/1¼ cups) of the cigar blanching water into a pan. Add the kappa and sugar and bring to the boil. Add the whisky and bring to a boil. Place in a small container, 3mm (⅛ inch) tall, and leave to set. Once set, cut the gelatine into small cubes 3mm (⅛ inch) on each side. Set aside.

Gather

4 cigars

16 litres (4 gallons) water

8 litres (2 gallons) sugar syrup at 30% (see below)

For the sugar syrup at 30%

6 litres (1½ gallons) water

1.8kg (4lb/8 cups) caster (superfine) sugar

Method

First make the sugar syrup. Place the water and sugar in a pan on a medium flame and bring to the boil until it is just dissolved. Remove the foam from the top, and set aside.

Put the cigars in a pan with 8 litres (2 gallons) of cold water. Bring to the boil and when it reaches boiling point, carefully remove the cigars and empty the water. Repeat this process with the remaining 8 litres (2 gallons) of water.

Finally, place the sugar syrup in a pan together with the blanched cigars and cook for 15 minutes on a medium heat.

Unroll the cigars, extending their leaves on a silicone mat or on a tray lined with baking paper, and leave to dry at 40°C (100°F) for 24 hours.

CHOCOLATE CRUNCH

Gather

460g (1lb) of tant pour tant – this is a sugar syrup made of 50% water and 50% caster sugar

240g (8½oz) glucose

480g (1lb 1oz/4¼ cups) raw cacao powder

Method

Preheat the oven to 170°C (325°F/gas mark 3). Warm the tant pour tant and glucose in a pan over a low heat, until it reaches 60°C (140°F). Add the cacao powder and mix well with the help of a hand blender. Spread the mixture out at 1mm (less than ⅛ inch) thickness over a silicone mat or on a tray lined with baking paper. Cook in a dry oven for 10 minutes. Set aside.

TO SERVE

Gather

Vanilla powder

Amarena cherries (pitted and quartered)

40% chocolate (preferably Rocolat by Cacao Barry), room temperature

VANILLA AND CHERRY VINAIGRETTE

Gather

100ml (3½fl oz/scant ½ cup) vanilla oil (see below)

100g (3½oz/½ cup) of morello cherry purée (preferably Boiron)

For the vanilla oil

500ml (18fl oz/2 cups) sunflower oil

5 vanilla pods

Method

First, make the vanilla oil. Put both ingredients in a vacuum bag and seal. Cook at 60°C (140°F) in a Roner water bath for 1 hour.

When the vanilla oil is ready, mix the measured amount with the cherry purée and set aside.

Method

First, make chocolate shavings. Using a vegetable peeler in short motions, scrape chocolate shavings from the bar.

In the centre of a plate, place one large dollop of the plum and tobacco purée and another three smaller dollops around it. Pop cubes of whisky and cigar water gelatine on the smaller dollops.

CARAMELISED WALNUTS

Gather

100ml (3½fl oz/scant ½ cup) water

60g (2¼oz/⅓ cup) caster (superfine) sugar

100g (3½oz/¾ cup) walnuts

40g (1½oz/⅓ cup) icing (powdered) sugar

Sunflower oil, for deep-frying

Method

Place the water and sugar in a pan and bring to the boil. Add the walnuts and cook on a low heat until they are very tender, almost translucent. Strain and leave to dry on a silicone mat. Cut each walnut into quarters and cover with the icing sugar. Deep-fry in sunflower oil at 180°C (350°F) until golden brown and crunchy. Remove from the oil and place on kitchen towel. Set aside.

Place the parfait on the large central dollop. Sprinkle one corner with the vanilla powder. Place four caramelised walnut pieces and two Amarena cherry quarters on the other corner of the parfait.

Drizzle a very fine line of vanilla and cherry vinaigrette around the plate. Finally, place the chocolate shavings, chocolate crunch and the crystallised cigar leaves on top of the parfait.

Gather

100g (3½oz) sugar

1 pomegranate

Just over 2 shots (60ml/2.4oz) dry oloroso sherry

Just under 1 shot (20ml/0.8oz) single cream

Just under 1 shot (20ml/0.8oz) walnut liqueur

1 shelled walnut, to garnish

SILK SLIP COCKTAIL

Oloroso, walnut liqueur, cream, pomegranate caramel

Suitably luxurious, this is a creamy drink that doesn't feel too heavy – it sits alongside dessert, rather than being a replacement for one.

Method

Pomegranate caramel (makes enough for several serves):
Add sugar to a pan and heat over a medium heat until it begins to caramelise. As it begins to smell deliciously golden, squeeze in the juice of a pomegranate (cut it into eighths and use your lemon squeezer, then it's easy – just be careful as it will hiss and spit like a demon). Remove from the heat, and whisk to dissolve the caramel.

To serve:
Shake 1 tablespoon pomegranate caramel with sherry, cream and liqueur without ice. Shake with cubed ice, then strain into a chilled cocktail glass. Garnish with crushed walnut.

The simplicity of this pasta dish hides how excellent it can be. The satisfaction of a bowl of delicious carbs elevated to the level of Tim's cooking is sensational, and to match it I've created a comforting riff on wine that will help you sink into the sofa even deeper.

PASTA AND 'WINE'

with Tim Siadatan, Trullo, padella

EYE OF THE PARTRIDGE

Vin santo, chestnut, cherry and juniper vinegar
(pictured previous page)

Gather

5 cherries

10 juniper berries

2 shots (50ml/2oz) red wine vinegar

2 shots (50ml/2oz) vin santo

2 tsp chestnut liqueur

Cocktail cherries, to garnish

Method

De-stone cherries, and muddle in a jar with juniper berries and red wine vinegar. Rest in a dark place for 2 days, agitating regularly, then strain.

In a mixing glass, stir over cubed ice the vin santo and chestnut, along with 4 dashes cherry and juniper vinegar. Strain into a chilled wine glass, and garnish with a skewered cherry.

HIGHLAND FIRE WATER

Clynelish, Ardmore, walnut oil, maple and red grape

Gather

5 sage leaves

4 shots (100ml/4oz) walnut oil

4 shots (100ml/4oz) Ardmore Legacy

4 shots (100ml/4oz) Clynelish 14

25g (1oz) unsalted butter

75g (3oz) soft brown sugar

50g (1¾oz) walnuts

2 shots (50ml/2oz) red grape juice

1 tsp maple syrup

2 dashes Peychaud's bitters

2 dashes Angostura bitters

Pinch salt

Method

Fat-washed whiskies:
Take sage leaves and gently fry them in the walnut oil until crisp. Allow to cool, then strain the oil into a narrow container filled with the whiskies. Shake, then transfer to the freezer. Allow the oil to solidify, then skim, and strain through a coffee filter. Keep cool – this will make enough for a few rounds.

Candy walnuts:
Melt butter in a pan and add the sugar. Allow to melt and caramelise, then toss in the walnuts. Coat well, then transfer to a baking sheet and allow to cool. Separate so they don't clump together.

To serve:
In a mixing glass, stir over cubed ice the grape juice with 1 shot (25ml/1oz) whisky mix, the maple syrup, bitters and salt. Strain over a big cube of ice in a chilled rocks glass, and sit a piece of caramelised walnut on the top.

Serves 4

2 grouse

½ onion, finely chopped

1 celery stick, finely chopped

1 carrot, finely chopped

2 garlic cloves, finely chopped

2 plum tomatoes, peeled and deseeded

1 tbsp roughly chopped thyme, juniper and bay leaves (tied up in a muslin)

½ tsp freshly ground cinnamon

175ml (6fl oz/¾ cup) red wine

300ml (10fl oz/1¼ cups) chicken stock

60g (2¼oz/¼ cup) unsalted butter, cubed

500g (1lb 2oz) pappardelle

Good-quality olive oil

Sea salt and freshly ground black pepper

60g (2¼oz/⅓ cup) finely grated parmesan, to serve

PAPPARDELLE WITH GROUSE RAGU

Ahh, grousey grouse – a uniquely flavored bird and one with the most street cred, so much so it has a day named after it to signify the start of the game season in August, fondly known as 'The Glorious Twelfth'. *Tim Siadatan*

Method

Preheat the oven to 180°C (350°F/gas mark 4).

Heat a pan large enough to fit both grouse in, on a medium heat, and add a touch of olive oil. Season the grouse with salt, then add to the pan. Cook until all sides of the birds have coloured (don't be tempted to rush this stage as this is where you'll create a lot of flavour). Once the grouse are beautifully golden, take the legs off the bird and put it all to one side.

Add a little more olive oil to the pan, then add the onion, celery, carrot, garlic, tomatoes, herbs and spices. Sweat for 25–30 minutes on a medium-low heat until they are totally soft. Add the wine, increase the heat to medium-high and cook for 5 minutes until slightly reduced. Add the chicken stock and bring to the boil, then season with salt and pepper. Transfer everything (including the grouse) to a casserole dish, add a glug of excellent-quality olive oil and put the lid on, or tightly seal with tin foil. Roast for 20 minutes and take out the crowns/breast of the birds and continue cooking the legs and vegetables for another 40 minutes. Take the legs out and set aside.

Put the cooking liquid with all its grousey goodness back on the hob, on a medium-high heat, and reduce until it thickens slightly. Take off the heat to cool, then remove the muslin of herbs and spices.

Pull the breast off the crown and the meat off the legs and chop it all into small pieces (be careful of lead shot and small bones). Stir into the thickened sauce and add a good grind of pepper and salt, if necessary. You can chill in the fridge for up to 2 days.

To serve, bring water to the boil in a pan (following pappardelle packet instructions) and add salt. Heat the grouse ragu and the butter in a large saucepan, big enough to fit the cooked pappardelle as well. Cook the pappardelle for 1 minute less than instructed on the packet, then strain it, but be sure to retain the pasta water. Add the pappardelle to the ragu and stir vigorously over a medium heat, adding small ladlefuls of the pasta water as you go, to emulsify the sauce. The aim is an unctuous, silky sauce that hugs the pasta ribbons. Serve on hot plates and finish with grated parmesan on top.

HOME COMFORTS

with Nuno Mendes, Chiltern Firehouse, Taberno do Mercado

Nuno's oyster and onion dish is the perfect thing to hunker down with on a cold night – and it pairs perfectly with a larger cocktail. Start with a Bosom Caresser for extra cosiness. Ahem.

BOSOM CARESSER

Madeira, cognac, grenadine, salt and orange egg

This classic cocktail puzzled me for a long time, as it just didn't balance properly, until I found the very dry Sercial madeira. The orange egg is a simple twist on truffled eggs: using the egg's porosity and ability to absorb flavours, you can scent it with anything with a strong flavour. Here the orange peel adds a lovely background brightness. I'm not sure where the classic Bosom Caresser name originates from, but it's certainly a comforting drink that's a perfect precursor to a comforting meal. I made a version of this when I worked at Whistling Shop cocktail bar called the Substitute Bosom Caresser – it used formula milk (a vanilla-like milk powder) in lieu of egg, and it's the only time I've noticed a difference in terms of gender reception (the female guests were quite put off by it, guys didn't seem to even notice, or care).

Gather

Serves 2

1 orange

1 egg

1 pinch salt

1 shot (25ml/1oz) 10yo dry madeira

1 shot (25ml/1oz) VSOP cognac

1 tbsp real grenadine

Cocktail cherries, to garnish

Method

Wrap the egg in the peel of the orange and leave to infuse in a cold, dark place for a day or two. For extra flavour, keep the wrapped egg in a closed container.

When ready, crack the orange egg into a cocktail shaker and add the salt, madeira, cognac and grenadine. Shake without ice, then shake with ice and double strain into a pair of small cocktail glasses. Garnish with a cherry in each.

PEAK BIERE

Amaro, Cointreau, pink grapefruit and Lyan Lager

Use a lightly hoppy beer with a bright fruitiness if you can't get our wonderful Lyan Lager!

Gather

Serves 2

Just over 1 shot (30ml/1oz) Zucca amaro

Just over 1 shot (30ml/1oz) Cointreau

1 strip grapefruit peel (optional)

1 330ml can Lyan Lager (or similar)

Method

Stir all the ingredients (except the beer) over ice, then strain into two chilled wine glasses. Top up each glass with the lager.

OYSTERS AND ONIONS

Comfort food should be about minimum effort for maximum effect and I think this soup hits the spot! Inspired by a dish I used to order from one of my favourite local Lisbon haunts, it has all the elements you want – rich flavour, wholesome body and a hint of decadence. *Nuno Mendes*

Gather

Serves 4

3 tbsp olive oil, plus extra to drizzle on the bread when toasting

40g (1½oz/2¾ tbsp) butter

4 medium white onions, thinly sliced

4 medium brown onions, thinly sliced

4 medium shallots, thinly sliced

Ground white pepper and sea salt

20ml (1½ tbsp) brandy, plus extra, to taste, once cooked

50ml (2fl oz/3½ tbsp) madeira, plus extra, to taste, once cooked

800ml (1½ pints/3¼ cups) chicken stock

60ml (4 tbsp) single (light) cream

A splash of sherry vinegar

4 slices of bread (I like to use a sourdough or white country loaf), thickly sliced

8 oysters (rock oysters or native oysters recommended, as fresh as possible)

50g (1¾oz) Parmesan (or similar hard cheese), grated

Cracked black pepper, to serve

Glug of extra virgin olive oil, to serve

Method

Heat the olive oil and butter in a large saucepan on a medium heat. When the pan is hot, add the onions and shallots. Season generously with ground white pepper and sea salt. Stir well to ensure they are thoroughly coated in the oil and butter. Using a large pan allows them to cook gently without browning them. When you cook them like this, they will become juicy and release a beautiful sweet flavour.

Pour the brandy and madeira into the pan and mix well with the onions and shallots. Cook for a few minutes, then add the chicken stock. Cover with a lid and leave to simmer gently for 45 minutes on a low heat. Halfway through the cooking time, take the lid off and stir – if they are starting to catch, add a little water.

After 45 minutes or when the onions and shallots are sweet and juicy, take the pan off the heat. Remove roughly 1 tablespoon of onions/shallots per person from the pan and set aside in a bowl. Now add the cream to the remaining mix in the pan. At this stage you can also use a hand blender to blend the soup smooth if you prefer. Taste to check the seasoning – you can add a little more brandy, madeira, a dash of sherry vinegar, salt and pepper to boost the flavours.

Preheat the oven to 200°C (400°F/gas mark 6). Place the slices of bread on a baking tray and drizzle generously with olive oil on each side. Cook in the oven for 5 minutes or until the bread is golden brown and crispy.

I find this dish easiest to eat out of wide, shallow bowls. Serve the shucked oysters on the toast on the side and add the oyster juice to the soup. I like to then add a little puddle of soup to the toast to warm the oysters slightly, just before serving. Dot with a spoonful of the reserved cooked onions/shallots and finish with a little grated Parmesan, a glug of extra virgin olive oil and cracked black pepper.

This is not an everyday feast, and although you could focus instead on individual recipes, it becomes incredible when you combine them (together they'll serve a party of four). Plus you get to scare the hell out of your friends with a fish head.

SMALL PLATES

with Robin Gill, The Dairy, The Manor, paradise Garage, Counter Culture

Gather

3cm (1.1 inch) dried kombu

500ml (20oz) grain whisk(e)y

1 tbsp peach brandy

Just under 1 shot (20ml/0.8oz) lemon juice

1 tsp sugar syrup

Pinch/knife-point matcha powder

1 egg white

Tomato powder

Method

Kombu whisky:
Take a the strip of dried kombu and infuse in the grain whisky for 1 hour, then strain. (You'd think kombu would add a savoury edge, but in fact it lifts the green fruitiness of the whisky.)

To serve:
Add the peach brandy, lemon, sugar, matcha, egg white and just under 2 shots (40ml/1.6oz) kombu-infused whisky to a shaker. Shake all without ice, then shake with cubed ice. Double strain into a chilled cocktail glass and dust with a little tomato powder. You can buy tomato powder online, and it gives a little vegetal contrast to the drink. Omit if necessary.

COLLAR & CUFF

Grain whisky, kombu, peach, lemon, matcha, tomato powder

There are some great grain whiskies about now – from Scotland, Japan and Ireland and further afield. Stick with a light, fruity and clean style, rather than the venerable versions – although delicious, they'd swamp both the other delicate flavours in the drink, and the feel of the meal.

Gather

Serves 4, but can be scaled up

4 shots (100ml/4oz) Mr Lyan Cream Gin (or a creamy-style London Dry)

2 shots (50ml/2oz) sweet vermouth

1 shot (25ml/1oz) raspberry syrup

1 can Guinness Draught

BAT'S NOSE

Cream gin, raspberry, vermouth, Guinness

Method

Stir the gin, vermouth and syrup over ice and strain into 4 chilled flutes, then top with the Guinness.

This twist on a Dog's Nose is an ideal group serve with these dishes. The rich creaminess with a light metallic edge is superb with fish and seafood. It's named after my black-and-white cat Batman and his pink nose, rather than the caped crusader.

COD HEAD, NORI AND POTATO SANDWICH

Gather

1 litre (1¾ pints/4 cups) water

70g (2½oz/¼ cup) salt

1 cod head (about 800g/1lb 12oz)

50g (1¾oz) dried wakame

80ml (3fl oz) rice wine vinegar mixed with 100ml (3½fl oz) water

80g (3oz) sugar

6 large Agria potatoes

Vegetable oil, for deep-frying

60g (2oz/½ cup) crème fraîche

5g (1¾ tsp) dried nori powder

Method

Mix the water and salt to make a brine. Add the cod head, leave for 6 hours.

Add the sugar to the rice wine vinegar/water mix and bring to the boil. Put the wakame in a small bowl and pour over the sugar solution. Allow to cool. This will keep in the fridge for a week.

Cut the potatoes lengthways into slices about 1cm (½ inch) thick. Select the largest 12, and set everything else aside for another recipe. Deep-fry the 12 slices until golden on the outside.

When ready to eat, remove the cod's head from the brine and cook gently in a bamboo steamer for 20 minutes. When cooked, the meat should fall away from the bone – toss the meat in a bowl with the crème fraîche and nori powder. To serve, sandwich the dressed cod and the pickled wakame between slices of fried potato.

MISO BBQ COD COLLAR TACOS

Gather

1 litre (1¾ pints/4 cups) water

70g (2½oz/¼ cup) salt

2 cod collars

30g (1oz) dried wakame

20g (¾oz/1⅓ tbsp) brown miso paste

50g (1¾oz/2⅓ tbsp) honey

1 bunch of sorrel

30g (1oz/4 tbsp) crème fraîche

Method

Mix the water and the salt to make a brine. Add the whole cod collars, and leave for 6 hours.

When you are ready to eat, fry the dry wakame over a low heat with a touch of oil for 1–2 minutes. Drain on kitchen paper.

Mix the miso and honey together and rub deep into the collars. Put them on the BBQ for 2 minutes each side (or on a griddle pan over a high heat). Remove from the heat and separate into large flakes of fish.

Select the largest and freshest leaves from the bunch of sorrel to use like taco carriers. Serve one flake of fish on each leaf, with a dollop of crème fraîche, fermented fennel (see recipe on page 181) and fried wakame.

SMOKED COD ROE

Gather

10g (¼oz) dried kombu

20ml (1⅓ tbsp) grapeseed oil

1 large very fresh cod roe

20g (¾oz/1⅓ tbsp) apple wood chips, for smoking

80g (2¾oz/⅔ cup) crème fraîche

1 bunch of fresh radishes

Salt

Method

First, make kombu oil. Preheat the oven to 180°C (350°F/gas mark 4). Cut the kombu into small pieces and roast for 10 minutes. Blend the cooked kombu with the oil for 2 minutes, using a hand blender. Leave to infuse for an hour, then pass through a fine sieve.

Cut the membrane off the roe and rinse the roe in cold water for 5 minutes. Drain, then weigh it. Add 2.5% salt (ie if you have 100g of roe, add 2½g salt). Mix the salt with the roe. Leave for 6 hours. When ready, heat the chips in a tray then set a steam tray above. Put the roe in a bowl, and put the bowl on top of another bowl, before placing on the steam tray and covering; cold-smoke for 10 minutes.

Mix the roe with the crème fraîche, and drizzle the kombu oil on top. Serve with a side of radishes and a pinch of rock salt.

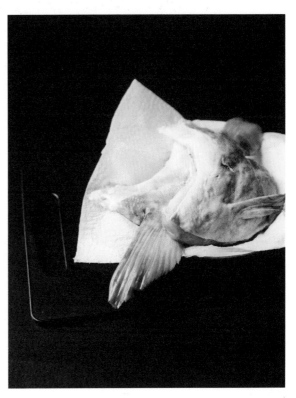

Gather

250ml (9fl oz/1 cup) water

250ml (9fl oz/1 cup) white wine vinegar

150g (5½oz/¾ cup) caster (superfine) sugar

8 coriander seeds

8 black peppercorns

1 cinnamon stick

1 star anise

2 cloves

Pinch of mace

Salt, 0.5% weight of all above ingredients' total weight

4 ripe white peaches (peeled)

LAST YEAR'S PICKLED WHITE PEACHES

Method

Combine all the ingredients except the peaches into a pan and simmer for 5 minutes. Place the peaches in a sterilised Kilner jar and pour the hot liquid over the top. Seal the jar and leave for at least 7 days before using.

This (together with the fermented fennel below) is an excellent condiment for the cod tacos – they can be laid out on the table to allow people to build their own. *Robin Gill*

FERMENTED FENNEL

Gather

15g (½oz/1 tbsp) fennel seeds

20 black peppercorns

6 star anise

1 tsp cumin seeds

10 pink peppercorns

6 fennel bulbs

1 garlic cloves, sliced

Apple juice

Salt

Method

First, gently toast each spice separately in a dry frying pan over a low heat. Leave to cool, then combine and grind to a powder.

Trim the tops of the fennel bulbs and put in a juicer, along with the outer pieces. Put the resulting juice in a measuring jug. Add 50% apple juice. For example, if you have 50ml (2fl oz) fennel juice, add 25ml (1fl oz) of apple juice.

Chop the remaining fennel and place in a sterilised jar. Add the juice, toasted spice powder and the sliced garlic. Top the jar with water or whey to cover the fennel, if needed. Weigh the contents of the jar and add 2% salt. Seal the jar and shake well to distribute the salt and spices. Leave somewhere warm, for about 2 weeks, shaking the jar a few times in the first 5 days of fermenting.

Food and drink are even better when shared, so why not get your pals involved directly with DIY wontons and cocktails.

BUILD YOUR OWN

with Isaac McHale, The Clove Club

I don't cook for friends enough – the chef's curse, but I do love a casual sit-around where everyone gets to help. Making dumplings together is perfect for a friends' night in. It's easy to do, you can be a little competitive, you can have fun with different shapes and you can blether while having a drink. The filling options are endless. Here, I suggest three. A veggie one with chopped spinach and peanuts, a minced chicken and pork one, and a prawn and mushroom one. *Isaac McHale*

DUMPLINGS

Gather

Serves 10

3 packets yellow wonton wrappers

3 packets white wonton wrappers

For the chicken and pork filling

1 chicken breast (about 300g/10½oz), skin off, diced

500g (1lb 2oz) pork belly, skin off, diced

½ garlic clove, crushed

5g (⅛oz/1 tbsp) ginger, finely chopped

40ml (3 tbsp) shaoxing Chinese rice wine or dry sherry

20ml (1⅓ tbsp) soy sauce (preferably Kikkoman brand)

15g (½oz/1 tbsp) sea salt

For the vegetarian filling

2kg (4½lb) spinach, preferably in bunches so you can use leaves and stems

200g (7oz/1⅓ cups) peanuts, skinless, lightly toasted and crushed

15g (½oz/3 tbsp) ginger, finely chopped

100g (3½oz) (rehydrated weight) dried and rehydrated shiitake mushrooms, finely chopped

1 tbsp soy sauce

20ml (1⅓ tbsp) olive oil

Salt and white pepper

For the prawn (shrimp) and mushroom filling

200g (7oz/1¾ cups) button mushrooms, finely chopped

150g (5½oz) (rehydrated weight) dried and rehydrated shiitake mushrooms, finely chopped

30ml (2 tbsp) olive oil

10g (¼oz/2 tbsp) ginger, finely chopped

½ garlic clove, finely chopped

1kg (2lb 4oz) peeled raw tiger prawns (shrimps)

15g (½oz/1 tbsp) salt

20ml (1⅓ tbsp) tamari (shoyu sauce)

For the dipping sauces

Plain soy sauce

1 tsp mirin

200ml (7fl oz/¾ cup) soy sauce

Spicy sauce

100ml (3½fl oz/scant ½ cup) soy sauce

75g (2½oz) gochujang paste

60ml (4 tbsp) water

15ml (1 tbsp) sesame oil

Vinegar sauce

60ml (4 tbsp) black vinegar

20ml (1⅓ tbsp) soy sauce

20ml (1⅓ tbsp) olive oil

Method

Prepare the fillings and sauces. First, make the chicken and pork filling. Mix all the ingredients together, leave for 1 hour to cure, then pulse in a food processor to mince. Chill in the fridge until you are ready to use it.

Next, make the vegetarian filling. Blanch the whole leaves of spinach with stems in boiling salted water, for a full 30 seconds. Refresh in iced water and drain. Squeeze hard to remove the excess water, then chop. Squeeze again and put into a large bowl. Add the peanuts, ginger, a pinch of salt and twist of white pepper. Moisten the chopped shiitake with the soy sauce and add it to the bowl. Add the olive oil, then taste and adjust the seasoning. Chill in the fridge until you are ready.

Next, make the prawn and mushroom filling. Sweat the button and shiitake mushrooms in the olive oil, with a pinch of salt, over a low heat. Add the ginger and garlic and cook with the mushrooms until the mushrooms are soft. Leave to cool down. Pulse the raw prawn, salt and tamari in a blender until you have a paste, then mix in the cool mushrooms. Chill in the fridge until you are ready.

Finally, make the dipping sauces. For the plain soy sauce, add the mirin to the soy sauce to make it less salty. Or you can add a splash of water instead, if there is no mirin to hand. Mix together the ingredients for the other sauces and refrigerate until needed.

Make the dumplings
Buy a load of steamer baskets from a Chinese supermarket. Lightly oil the bases. Cut a small circle of baking paper for each, fold in six, and cut out some shapes like you were making snowflakes. Put in the bases so the dumplings don't stick. Make sure the paper is smaller than the base of the steamer so steam can still get in.

Set up a few empty plates or trays for the finished dumplings. Place the three filling mixes in the middle of the table and a stack of wrappers next to each. Stick a few teaspoons in each mix so people can use them, and dot a few coffee cups a third full of water around the table, for people to dip their fingers in to seal the dumplings.

Watch some YouTube videos to show you how to fold the dumplings. Have a go at various shapes: the simple triangle fold, the beggar's purse, tortellini and gyoza shapes. Get the drinks poured and get everyone folding.

Once you have made enough, get a few boiling pots going and steamer baskets filled ready to cook.

Clean the table, saving any leftover mixes in clean bowls, covered, in the fridge. Wrap any extra wonton skins in cling film and keep in the fridge too.

Get the dips on the table and get steaming! They'll take about 12 minutes on hard steam; don't stack the baskets any more than five high. And don't let the water boil dry!

I would also steam some choi sum in between rounds of dumplings, and maybe even buy some spicy Thai prawn crackers, the kind you fry at home, to deep-fry as a little perk in between dumplings.

Happy eating.

Gather

Makes 1 bottle

100g (3½oz) sugar

6 cubes fresh or tinned pineapple

Half a vanilla pod

Pinch salt

6 black peppercorns

1 tsp coriander seed

400ml (14oz) citrus vodka

Berries – bowls of strawberries, raspberries, blackberries

Citrus – wedges of lime, lemon, orange, grapefruit

Herb – bunches of basil, mint, rosemary, thyme

Bitters – dasher bottles of orange bitters, Angostura

Tabasco

Mixers – chilled bottles of soda, ginger ale, ginger beer, fresh lemonade

BOTTLE DAISY

Citrus vodka, vanilla pineapple sizzurp and DIY hi-balls

Make it easy! This recipe makes a batch in a bottle so its tailor-made for sharing. As for the rest, the berries don't need muddling, the herbs are aromatic, and the fruits add a nice sharpness to balance things out… but it's by no means exhaustive! Just use things that don't require additional tools.

Method

Vanilla pineapple sizzurp:
Heat a pan with 120ml (4.8oz) water and bring to the boil. Remove from the heat and immediately add the sugar, pineapple, vanilla – seeds scraped into the pot – salt, peppercorns and coriander seed. Swirl about, allow to infuse as it cools, then strain.

In a clean bottle, mix the vodka with cold syrup. Keep cold until ready to use.

To serve:
On the table set a big bowl of ice and some small rocks and hi-ball glasses along with the bottle, ingredients and some teaspoons and chopsticks. Chopsticks are better than spoons for getting in among the ice and giving your drink a stir. Use the basic formula below, but allow people to chop and change according to taste:

2 shots bottle mix + 2 squeezes citrus + dash bitters + a couple of berries, and mixer. Garnish with (spanked) herb.

Angela is a master of big flavours that somehow harmonise without overwhelming your palate. It's big-flavoured, fun food, with big-flavoured, fun twists in the drinks!

A SHARING FEAST

with Angela Dimayuga, Mission Chinese Food

1 cox apple

1 tsp ascorbic acid dissolved in half a litre of water (vitamin C powder)

150g (5½oz) white sugar

A shot-and-a-half (35ml/1.4oz) whole or semi-skimmed fresh milk

Just over 2 shots (60ml/2.4oz) Mr Lyan Cream Gin (or similar)

Just under 1 shot (20ml/0.8oz) lime juice

Chocolate bitters

Method

Apple balls:
Cut melon balls (you know what I mean) out of a firm apple – cox is ideal. Plunge immediately into a solution with citric or ascorbic acid to prevent it going brown.

Milk syrup:
Heat a pan with 4 shots (100ml/4oz) water (fresh, without the acid in it), the white sugar and the milk. Bring to the boil (careful, it'll rise up!), and skim the foamy fat that forms in the middle. Boil for 3 minutes continuing to skim, collecting all the white milky solids, then allow to cool.

To serve:
Add to a shaker: the Cream Gin, the lime juice, 1 tablespoon of the milk syrup and 2 dashes chocolate bitters. Shake with ice, then double strain into a cocktail glass, and garnish with the apple ball.

MILK GIMLET

Cream Gin, chocolate bitters, lime, 'blue' milk syrup, apple ball

My Mr Lyan Cream Gin adds a rich, smooth weight to this drink, but use a classic London Dry if unavailable. The milk syrup goes a light blue – a symptom of the casein reflecting more blue wavelengths, but it's still safe to use!

1 pitted Mission, Nyon or
Beldi black olive

3 leaves sea purslane or a
sprig of samphire

1 shot (25ml/1oz) London Dry Gin

Just over 1 shot (30ml/1oz) rich,
vanilla-led sweet vermouth

1 shot (25ml/1oz) Campari

1 dash Peychaud's bitters

Black sesame cracker, to garnish

SEASIDE NEGRONI

*Gin, black olive, sea purslane, Peychaud's,
vermouth, Campari, black sesame candy*

Method

In the bottom of a mixing glass,
muddle one olive along with a few
leaves of sea purslane (or the sprig of
samphire) then add the gin, vermouth
and both bitters. Stir over ice briefly,
then double strain over ice in the rocks
glass and garnish with a black sesame
candy cracker.

Serves 4

12 little gem lettuce leaves

12 large mint leaves

12 Thai basil leaves

12 red shiso leaves

12 green shiso leaves

1cm (½ inch) piece of Thai chilli

1cm (½ inch) piece of Holland chilli

4 tbsp high-quality fish sauce

1 tbsp fresh lime juice

175g (6oz) flank steak, cut into ½cm (¼ inch) dice

3 tbsp crispy fried shallots

1 tbsp olive oil

55g (2oz/¼ cup) cured salmon roe, or trout roe

Freshly ground black pepper

Crushed ice, to serve (optional)

LETTUCE CUPS

An elegant lettuce cup made from stacked leaves and herbs. Guests spoon the tartare on to the cups themselves so the lettuce and herbs remain crisp. *Angela Dimayuga*

Method

Prepare the lettuce cups. Slice about 1cm (½ inch) off the base of the little gem lettuce head. Select 12 of the best full little gem lettuce leaves and put the rest and the hearts aside for another recipe. Place one lettuce leaf in your hand as the base for your layered lettuce cup. Stack, from bottom to top, one leaf of mint, Thai basil, red shiso and green shiso. Carefully arrange the stacked leaves on a tray and store in the fridge, covered with a damp cloth, to keep the herbs fresh and crisp while you prepare the tartare.

With a pestle and mortar, grind the chillies into a fine paste. Add the fish sauce, lime juice and a grind of black pepper to the mortar, and leave to marinate while you prepare the rest of the ingredients.

Put the diced steak into a small mixing bowl. Add the crispy fried shallots and olive oil, and as much of the lime and fish sauce dressing as you like, to taste. Mix to combine. The tartare should be bright and nicely seasoned with the dressing.

Transfer to a small serving bowl, and top with the roe. Rest the bowl on a larger platter on a bed of crushed ice. Arrange the lettuce cups around the ice. Guests can serve themselves by picking up a stack and adding a spoonful of the tartare.

CLAMS IN BLACK BEAN SAUCE

Clams and cockles are steamed in ham fat, white wine and aromatics, then the sauce is thickened with blood. A cross between Chinese clams and a Filipino pork blood stew. *AD*

Gather

Serves 4

2 tbsp rendered Iberico ham fat

2 tbsp olive oil, plus extra to serve

1 rosemary sprig

1 bay leaf

1 garlic clove, crushed

1 tsp fresh chilli, finely chopped

1 tsp Chinese fermented
black bean paste

680g (1½lb) manila clams, purged

680g (1½lb) cockles, purged

125ml (4fl oz/½ cup) white wine

½ tsp squid ink

3 tbsp pork blood (see note in method)

1 lemon, deseeded and cut
into 4 wedges

15 Thai basil, red shiso and
green shiso leaves, to serve

Method

Heat a large sauté pan with a lid on a high heat until smoking. Add the ham fat, olive oil, rosemary, bay leaf, garlic, chilli and black bean paste. Agitate until fragrant, about 30 seconds, then carefully transfer the clams and cockles to the pan without breaking any shells. Immediately add the white wine, cover with the lid and steam for 2 minutes, agitating occasionally. Remove the lid and the shellfish should be partially opened. Decrease the heat to medium and add the squid ink and pork blood to thicken the sauce. Toss a couple times on and off the heat, being careful not to scorch the sauce and break the emulsification.

Note: the pork blood is here for depth, a rich iron flavour and texture (it's an emulsifier and thickening agent). For substitutions, you can use lardo, cured pork belly, guanciale and other types of cured pork fat. Bacon would be too smoky and aggressive.

Once the sauce is emulsified, turn the heat off and check the thickness of the sauce. It should coat the back of a spoon. Squeeze two lemon wedges into the sauce and toss, then transfer to a bowl to serve.

To finish the clams, drizzle with olive and garnish with the herbs.

Serve with lots of napkins and an extra bowl for the empty shells.

UMESHISO FRIED RICE

I love getting an umeshiso handroll at the end of a Japanese omakase meal. This is inspired by that, but combined with a simple Filipino garlic rice. *AD*

Gather

Serves 4

2 tbsp butter

1 garlic clove, crushed

½ purple sweet potato, peeled, steamed, and crumbled into chunks

200g (7oz/scant 1 cup) jasmine rice, steamed

1 tbsp fried sliced garlic

12 shiso leaves, finely shredded

6 umeboshi, pitted and chopped into a coarse paste

Salt, to taste

Cucumber matchsticks, to garnish

Method

In a small saucepan, melt the butter with the garlic. Cook on a low heat until softened, about 5 minutes.

Heat the oil in a hot wok or large sauté pan, and add the butter and softened garlic. Add the sweet potato and rice, and season with salt. Gently mix to incorporate thoroughly.

Transfer the rice to a large plate, and garnish with fried garlic, cucumber and shiso. Scatter small amounts of the umeboshi over the rice. Serve as is, and stir thoroughly right before eating.

Serves 4

1cm (½ inch) piece of Thai chilli

1cm (½ inch) piece of Holland chilli

2 tbsp high-quality fish sauce
(eg Red Boat brand)

4 Hokkaido scallops or the freshest
best-quality scallops you can find

1 large piece of dried kombu

1 grapefruit

1 lime

A few pinches of shio kombu

Crushed ice, to serve (optional)

16 pieces of Korean gim nori
(roasted seaweed)

HOKKAIDO SCALLOPS WITH GRAPEFRUIT VINAIGRETTE

A fresh crudo to eat with your hands. I love Hokkaido scallops, which are so sweet and tender, paired with a fresh piece of grapefruit and dressed with lime and fish sauce. The scallops stick to the kombu as it cures, so to eat it, you just pick up the scallop with your fingertips and wrap it in Korean-toasted nori. *AD*

Method

With a pestle and mortar, grind the chillies into a fine paste. Add the fish sauce to the mortar, and leave to marinate while you prepare the rest of the ingredients.

Hold a very sharp knife under cold running water to moisten, then turn each scallop on its side and slice into thin coins, about 4 per scallop. Place each piece gently on to the kombu, so the seaweed can quickly cure the scallop.

Supreme the grapefruit (cut off the peel and remove segments from the membrane), then cut the supremes into 1cm (½ inch) pieces.

Using a small teaspoon, dress each scallop with a drop or two of the fish sauce and chilli mixture. Arrange a single piece of grapefruit on top, and follow with a generous squeeze of fresh lime juice, and a few small pieces of shio kombu.

To serve, place the sheet of kombu over crushed ice, and lay the nori on a serving plate. Guests should use their fingers to peel the scallop away from the kombu and wrap it in a piece of nori for a delicate and flavourful bite.

Family-style banquets exist in several cultures, and their sense of celebration and gathering suits small and big hordes alike. The spices Lisa uses give such an amazing complexity, and the drinks I've made are designed to work with the food. They're either fresh and aromatic, or with some fat to mellow the spice away. In combination, this means they help you start to notice new flavours in the food, while other stronger ones are tempered by the creaminess.

EASTERN BANQUET

with Lisa Lov, Tigermom

LITTLE DEVIL SMASH

Gin, white rum, triple sec, Thai basil and lime

Gather

Just under 1 shot (20ml/0.8oz) London dry gin (citrus-led like Bombay Sapphire)

Just under 1 shot (20ml/0.8oz) white rum (clean like Bacardi Carta Blanca)

Just under 1 shot (20ml/0.8oz) triple sec (a dry style like Merlet)

Just under 1 shot (20m/0.8oz) lime juice

1 tbsp sugar syrup

4 Thai basil leaves (failing that, regular basil and a dash of absinthe), and more to garnish

Method

Add all to a shaker, shake very hard with ice (you want to obliterate the basil!), double strain over cubed and cracked ice, and garnish with some basil leaves.

Gather

Serves 6

2 pigs' ears

1 onion, peeled and quartered

1 celery stick, cut into large chunks

1 carrot, cut into large chunks

A bunch of coriander (cilantro) stems or stems from other herbs you've used

10g (¼oz/2 tsp) salt, plus coarse salt for cleaning the ears

1½ litres (2½ pints/6 cups) water

25g (1oz/2½ tbsp) toasted sesame seeds

A bunch of coriander (cilantro), leaves only

Oil, for deep-frying

For the fried chilli paste (makes more than you need)

180ml (6¼fl oz/¾ cup) oil

110g (3¾oz/1 cup) sliced garlic cloves (at least 2 garlic bulbs)

110g (3¾oz/1 cup) sliced shallots (about 4 shallots)

95g (3½oz) whole mixed dried chillies

7g (1¾ tsp) light raw sugar

4g (¾ tsp) salt

15ml (1 tbsp) tamarind water

For the chilli oil dressing

30g (1oz/2 tbsp) fried chilli paste (see above)

40ml (1½fl oz/2½ tbsp) apple cider vinegar

15ml (1 tbsp) oil

4g (¾ tsp) sugar

4g (¾ tsp) salt

PIGS' EAR SALAD WITH CHILLI OIL AND SESAME

Method

First, clean the pigs' ears thoroughly by rubbing them with coarse salt and rinsing well under cold water. Put them in a pan with the onion, celery, carrot, herb stems and salt, and cover with the water. Over a high heat, boil the ears until they are soft enough to put your fingernails through them easily, approximately 1–1½ hours. Remove the ears from the water and place in the fridge to cool. Once cooled, cut the ears into strips of 4cm (1½ inches) long and ½cm (¼ inch) thin. Return half of these to the fridge and place the other half on a dehydrator tray and dry out at 65°C (150°F), either overnight, or until dried completely. Heat the oil for deep-frying over a medium–high heat to 210°C (410°F) and fry the dried pigs' ears until puffed, approximately 10 seconds. Allow to cool.

Now make the fried chilli paste. Heat the oil in a small saucepan over a medium heat. Fry the garlic until lightly browned, then remove with a slotted spoon. Do the same for the shallots. Fry the whole chillies (stems on) in the same oil, but briefly, for 2–3 seconds per batch. Remove and allow the oil to cool. In a blender, blitz the fried garlic, shallots and chillies roughly. Heat a few tablespoons of the oil in a pan over a medium heat and add the paste. Season with the sugar, salt and tamarind water. Leave to simmer gently in the oil for a few minutes, without letting the paste get darker – so just until the seasonings dissolve. Add more oil if needed to adjust the consistency to an oily, but thick, heavy paste.

When the paste is ready, make the chilli oil dressing. Mix 30g of the chilli paste with all the other ingredients, taste and adjust the seasoning if you like.

When ready to serve, mix the pigs' ears with the chilli oil dressing, sprinkle with the toasted sesame seeds and coriander leaves and let marinate for about 10 minutes before serving.

Gather

Serves 6

1 chicken breast, skin on

500ml (18fl oz/2 cups) water

15g (½oz/1 tbsp) salt

200g (7oz) chicken skin

30ml (2 tbsp) oil

300g (10½oz) wild mushrooms, brushed clean

2 small Thai red chillies, roughly chopped

1 garlic clove, roughly chopped

10g (¼oz/2½ tsp) sugar

40ml (1½fl oz/2½ tbsp) fish sauce

40ml (1½fl oz/2½ tbsp) lime juice

250g (9oz) mixed herbs and leaves – coriander (cilantro), mint, spinach, watercress (salad cress) and whatever else you like

50g (1¾oz/½ cup) shallots, sliced

Salt, to taste

SALAD OF POACHED CHICKEN AND WILD MUSHROOMS

Method

Brine the chicken breast in the water and salt overnight. Remove the chicken breast from the water and seal in a vacuum bag. Poach sous-vide at 58°C (137°F) for 45 minutes. If you don't have a sous-vide machine at home, then you can poach the chicken breasts in chicken stock. Bring the stock to a boil over high heat, in a saucepan, add the chicken breasts, cover, turn off the heat and remove the saucepan from the stove. Allow the breasts to poach in the hot chicken stock away from direct heat, approximately 30 minutes depending on the size of the breast.

Cool the chicken breast (in the bag if cooked sous-vide). When cool, shred the chicken breast and its skin using your fingers.

Preheat the oven to 180°C (350°F/gas mark 4). Spread the chicken skin flat on

baking paper on a baking sheet, and lay another layer of paper on top and another tray on top of that, compress the chicken skin between the layers. Bake in the oven until golden brown, about 25–30 minutes. Remove from the oven and cool and drain on kitchen towel.

Heat a frying pan over a high heat and add the oil, followed by the mushrooms, and sauté until just cooked. Season with salt to taste.

In a pestle and mortar, pound the chilli, garlic and sugar together to form a rough paste. Add the fish sauce and lime juice to make a dressing. Taste and adjust the seasoning if needed.

Mix the shredded chicken breast with the mixed herbs, sliced shallots and sautéed mushrooms. Crush in some of the crispy chicken skin and mix in the dressing.

MILK PUNCH

Gin, wormwood, fino, mango, pine nut and condensed milk, clarified

Gather

Makes 1 bottle

1 litre (2½ pints) mango juice

360g (12.7oz) condensed milk (1 tin)

15g (½oz/1 tbsp) citric acid

Peel of one lemon

Peel of one grapefruit

300ml (12oz) gin

1 pinch wormwood

Peel of one green apple

10g (0.4oz) dried mango

10g (0.4oz) toasted pine nuts

4 shots (100ml/4oz) fino sherry

Method

Mango curdle:
Add the mango juice, condensed milk, citric acid, citrus peels and 4 shots (100ml/4oz) water to a microwave safe container, mix, nuke for 6 minutes, then pour through a coffee filter.

Infused gin:
Infuse the gin with the wormwood, green apple peel, dried mango and toasted pine nuts for 5 minutes, then pour through a coffee filter.

To bottle:
Mix together the sherry, 3 shots (75ml/3oz) water, 250ml (9fl oz) infused gin and 400ml (14fl oz) mango curdle. Bottle and chill.

To serve:
Pour cocktail over ice in a rocks glass.

HOT AND SOUR TAMARIND BROTH WITH BITTER GREENS AND COCKLES

Gather

Serves 6

1 litre (1¾ pints/4 cups) chicken stock

4 lemongrass sticks

8 lime leaves

2 shallots, halved

2 small Thai red chillies

A small bunch of coriander (cilantro) stems or 4 coriander roots

150g (5½oz) bitter greens, such as chard, spinach, rappini or any other leafy green vegetable

2kg (4½lb) cockles (about 250)

2 small Thai red chillies, bruised

Tamarind water, to taste

Lime juice, to taste

Fish sauce, to taste

Chilli oil, to taste

Coriander (cilantro) leaves, to serve

Method

Bring the chicken stock to the boil. Bruise all of the aromatics in a pestle and mortar and add them to the stock with the coriander stems or roots. Reduce the heat, and simmer to infuse for 20 minutes.

Strain the aromatics from the stock and return the infused stock to a large pan over a high heat. Add the bitter greens and cook until they are tender, approximately 3–4 minutes. Once the greens are cooked, add the cockles and put the lid on for about 2 minutes, until all the cockles just open.

Remove from the heat and season the soup with the chillies, tamarind water, lime juice and fish sauce, so that it is hot, sour and salty. Garnish with chilli oil and fresh coriander.

ROASTED WHOLE CAULIFLOWER WITH BLACK PEPPER AND MUSHROOM SAUCE

Gather

Serves 6

400ml (14fl oz/1⅔ cups) salted mushroom juice (see below)

45ml (3 tbsp) oil

5 garlic cloves, finely chopped

20g (¾oz) kuzu (or cornstarch)

5g (1 tsp) coarsely ground black pepper

150g (5½oz) pulp from the salted mushroom juice (see below)

1 whole cauliflower

For the salted mushroom juice (makes more than you need)

2kg (4½lb) button mushrooms, roughly sliced

60g (2¼oz/4 tbsp) salt

Method

First make the salted mushroom juice. Mix the mushrooms and salt together and place in a sealed container for several hours to marinate. Squeeze the mushrooms through a muslin cloth over a bowl to obtain the juice. Reserve both juice and pulp.

Heat the oil in a small saucepan over a medium heat and fry the garlic until golden brown. Retain the garlic oil, and set the garlic aside for another recipe.

Preheat the oven to 180°C (350°F/gas mark 4).

Over a medium-high heat, bring 400ml (14fl oz) of the salted mushroom juice to the boil, add the kuzu and black pepper and simmer until thick. Transfer the sauce into a blender, add the garlic oil and 150g (5½oz) of the pulp from the salted mushroom juice, and blitz until smooth. Keep warm.

Bake the cauliflower whole until slightly charred on the outside and cooked through to the middle, around half an hour. Pour the sauce over the cauliflower and serve.

CRISPY RICE WITH GINGER AND SPRING ONION OIL

Gather

Serves 6

60g (2¼oz/1 cup) ginger, peeled and finely grated

60g (2¼oz) spring onions (scallions), finely chopped, plus extra to garnish

12g (¼oz/2½ tsp) salt, plus extra to garnish

80ml (2¾fl oz/⅓ cup) oil, plus 3 tbsp for frying

5 garlic cloves, finely chopped

600g (1lb 5oz) jasmine rice

Method

Mix the ginger, spring onions and salt together in a heatproof bowl. In a small saucepan, over a high heat, heat the oil until it starts to smoke slightly. Pour the oil carefully over the ginger and spring onion mix.

In a small saucepan, heat the 3 tablespoons of oil over a medium heat, and gently fry the garlic, stirring frequently until it becomes a light golden brown. Remove from the heat. Once cooled, strain the fried garlic from the oil. Reserve both.

Wash the rice several times until the water no longer appears to be starchy. Cook the rice in a rice cooker with an appropriate amount of water (if you want measurements, check out the packaging, but I usually do it by eye!).

In a frying pan or wok, large enough to fit the cooked rice in, heat some of the oil from frying the garlic over a medium-low heat. Pack the rice into the pan and flatten it out. Let the rice slowly crisp up on one side until golden brown, approximately 10–15 minutes. Check by lifting up one of the sides.

When it's golden brown, spoon the ginger and spring onion infused oil over the non-crispy side of the rice, add the fried garlic and sprinkle with a little salt. Carefully turn the rice onto a plate, so that the crispy side is exposed. Garnish with spring onion, if you like.

RED CURRY OF BRAISED PORK CHEEKS WITH BOILED PEANUTS AND CONFIT POTATOES

Gather

Serves 6

For the braised marinated pork cheeks

6 pork cheeks

700ml (1¼ pints/2¾ cups) water

700ml (1¼ pints/2¾ cups) soy sauce

760ml (1⅓ pints/3 cups) coconut cream

2 lemongrass sticks

4 kaffir lime leaves

1 shallot, halved

1 small Thai red chilli

A small bunch of coriander (cilantro) stems or 2 coriander roots

For the red curry base (makes more than you need)

100g (3½oz) dried long red chillies, soaked and deseeded

75g (2½oz/½ cup) chopped lemongrass (about 3 stalks)

45g (1½oz) coriander (cilantro) roots

75g (2½oz/½ cup) chopped shallots (about 3 shallots)

100g (3½oz/1 cup) roughly chopped garlic cloves (about 2 garlic bulbs)

50g (1¾oz) shrimp paste

5g (1 tsp) salt

1 tbsp oil or coconut oil

685g (1½lb) cracked cream (coconut cream which has simmered for a while so the fat has split from the cream)

Approx 500ml (18fl oz/2 cups) chicken stock, plus a few extra splashes

Fish sauce, palm sugar and tamarind water, to taste

Other ingredients

100g (3½oz/⅔ cup) peanuts, skin on

1 litre (1¾ pint/4 cups) water

15g (½oz/1 tbsp) salt

500g (1lb 2oz) potatoes, peeled and cubed

Oil or chicken fat

A bunch of Thai basil, to garnish

Method

First, make the braised marinated pork cheeks. Marinate the pork cheeks in the water and soy sauce overnight. The next day, drain them, and braise them in a pan over a medium heat with the coconut cream and the aromatics, until they are fork-tender.

Next, make the red curry base. Grind or pound the chilli, lemongrass, coriander roots, shallots, garlic, shrimp paste and salt together, either in a blender or with a pestle and mortar.

Heat a large pot with the oil or coconut oil over a medium-high heat. Cook the paste in the oil, stirring constantly, until aromatic, approximately 5–10 minutes. Add the cracked cream and cook, stirring frequently, until the paste releases cooked aromas, approximately 10–15 minutes. Add the stock and cook until you have a thick, creamy consistency, emulsifying with the cream, then bring it down to simmer and add a small amount of fish sauce and palm sugar to taste. Cool and store in the fridge. If there is too much fat on it, remove most of it for a different use. It can have a little bit of fat, but the curry should not be too greasy.

In a pressure cooker, combine the peanuts, water and salt, and cook on a medium heat for 30 minutes. Release the pressure, drain the peanuts and cool them in cold water.

Place the potatoes in a pan over a medium heat, and enough oil or chicken fat to cover. Simmer until the potatoes are tender.

In a large pan, put about 250g (9oz/1 cup) of the red curry base and loosen it up with a few splashes of chicken stock – just enough to achieve a thick, creamy consistency. Bring to a simmer over a medium heat. Place the pork cheeks, peanuts and potatoes in the sauce and stir them gently to coat everything with sauce.

Season with fish sauce and tamarind water until it tastes salty, sweet and rich, with a bit of acidity. Garnish with lots of Thai basil and serve.

PURPLE POTATO COLADA

Rum, purple sweet potato, coconut cream, pineapple, vanilla salt

Gather

1 purple sweet potato (about 300g/10½oz)

75g (2½oz) sugar

5g (1 tsp) ascorbic acid (vitamin C powder)

300ml (12oz) Bacardi Carta Blanca

4 shots (100ml/4oz) Bacardi Carta Oro

1 shot (25ml/1oz) pressed pineapple juice

1 tbsp Coco López coconut cream

1 pinch vanilla salt

Method

Sweet potato rum (makes enough for several serves):
Boil the purple sweet potato – skin on – in a shallow pan of water, covered, for 45 minutes or until soft. Remove from water, and while warm, remove skin and add to a blender with the sugar, ascorbic acid and rums. Blend until smooth, then pass through a sieve.

To serve:
Add the pineapple juice, coconut cream and vanilla salt to a shaker with just over 2 shots (60ml/2.4oz) sweet potato rum. Shake, then strain into a small hi-ball with cubes of ice.

Gather

24 dashes absinthe

10g (0.4oz) uncooked rice

3g (0.1oz) pink peppercorns

½g cinnamon bark

1 star anise

1½g (0.05oz) liquorice root

Pinch caraway seed

350ml (14oz) vodka

2 shots (50ml/2oz) apricot brandy

Just over a shot (30ml/1.2oz) rice milk

2 tsp sugar syrup

Method

Absinthe ice:
Fill ice cube tray with water. Add 4 dashes absinthe to each cube before it's set and freeze overnight.

Rice vodka (makes enough for several serves):
Add the rice to a pan and cook over a high heat until lightly browned and aromatic. Reduce heat then add the other spices. Add to the vodka and apricot, allow to infuse for 2 hours, then strain through a coffee filter.

To serve:
Add to a shaker 2 shots (50ml/2oz) of the rice vodka with the rice milk and sugar. Shake with (regular) ice, then strained into a ceramic cup with 1 cube of absinthe ice.

RICE, RICE & ICE
Roasted rice-infused vodka, rice, absinthe ice

INDEX

Thank you! Y'all the best!

Arielle / Robin & Jade / Maja / Dave Broom / Andy & Lauren / Jacob Briars / Daphnée Hor / Alex Ricard and Gabrielle de la Fouchardiere / Nick Morgan / Lian, Emma, David, Alex, Alex / Ben, Michael, Emma, Rosie & MoM / Gemma, Rachel, Alice / Michael Friedrich / Rob Rose / Dan, Stocky, James, Jenny, Aidan, Mikey, Alex & team Dandelyan / Ally & Terri / Juliet, Luke & Simone / Mike & Jas / Harper / Tris / Henrietta / Ben Seedlip / Ben & Sashana / Ben, Brian & Kiln / Wai Ting & Bao / Hannah, Davide & team Selfridges / Vivek Singh & Tina / Anna Hansen / Sukhinder, Raj, Dawn, Eddy, Jon, Billy, Alex & TWE / Todd Selby / Cindy Gallop / Newington Green Fruit & Veg / Killian & The Gannet / Billy & JJ / Ali Kurshat Altinsoy / Bethany Ham, Alicia & Walter / Denver Cramer / Sandrae & Gary / Laura, Clint & Imbibe / Fraz / Jane Ryan, Hannah & Drink Up / Ali & Joe / Claire & Dan / Claire & Chad / Victor Jerez / Johnny Drain / Yao Wong / Mark Murphy / Hayden Lambert / Lewis Jaffrey / Bobby / Daz Haldane / Stu Bale & MRAC / Tina DB / Louise McGuane / David Ramsden / Becky, Richard & scotchwhisky.com / Joey Kent / Jason Standing / Alex, Simone, Monica, Jim, Xav, Joerg & P(our) / Kipps / Leslie & Frank / Big Frank / Nick & Linn / Marcin / Addie / Serena Tierney / Danni Barry / Pamela Wiznitzer / Marco Noe / Katie, Jezza, Barney & Queenie / Ras & Adi / Flora / Steve / Penny Ferguson / Pauli / Stu & Christie / Jenna & Chris / Sam & Mickey / Simon, Sharon & 86 / Shev & Olly / Mayface / Rebekkah, Sean & Jack / Sarah & James Goggin / Allison / Ago /Melissa, Michelle, Stef, Gina +++ / Niall & Lucy / Baz / Fabs / Steve Ryan & Root + Bone /

Shay Ola / Davide & Bene / Darren & Nicole / Neil & Joel / Cam & S+C / Em Wheldon / Stu & Herb / Trine & Morten / Caroline Childerley / Emma Monkey / TOTC / Abi Clephane / Zoë & Jack / Sam Hodges & Brick Kitchen / Jake Burger / Marcis & Michael / Jane Parkinson / Nikita Spice / Alice Lascelles / Liam Davy / Dan Gasper / Ian McLaren / Mr T / Gail Ferguson / Dunk & Farah / David Piper / Philippa / Nadine Redzepi / Esben Holmboe Bang / Beth & Sam / Martin Morales / Sam Dinsdale / Brett & Elliot's / Francis & Bronwyn / Paisley / John Deragon / Cami & Struan / Nick Strangeway / Silvia Farago / Jo Ratcliffe / Ben & Magpie / Stephen & Sarah / Clerkenwellboy Tim / Thomas Kuuttanen / Dan Bartley / Ivy & Lynette / Kiel / Alan & Gelareh / Josh McNorton / Derek Elefson / Stacey Podell / Charlie & Elli / Lynn & Chris / Josh, Carina, Adam & Co. / Paul Mant / Dave Arnold / Marco Pierre White / Alice Farquhar / Ros / Kat Odell / Tommy D / Laura / Lizzie / Lucie / Grant Neave / Richard Jolly / Donald Colville / Sarah, Hannah, Ailana & Story PR / John Glaser & Compass Box / Elli / Roselle, Kieran, Jackie & B&A / Jo Lacey / Nat Wright, Will & Jenny / Team Lyan / Peter & Harry Mead / Talia & Punch/ Batman

Lee, Kate, Elvis, Kas, Nelson Matt, Katherine, Jen / Karan & Su / Chet & Mark / Robin & Sarah Gill / Isaac, Daniel, Jonny & Clove Club / Angela & Mission Chinese / James, John & Lyle's / Lisa, Tigermom, Rita Chen, Martha Freja Andreassen, Kyumin Hahn, James Bond-Kennedy / Doug & Silo / Nieves & Barrafina / Nuno / Richard / Roca Brothers & The Macallan / Signe / Tien, Kate & Ruby Colette /Tom & Meryl / Tim & Jordan / Rys

Antoine & Hannah / Jam & Tash / Bari / Sarah / Lizzie & Ben / Christina & Neil / Alex, Tanya & Oscar / Vik & Leo / Bob & Gloria / Barney / Iain & Kelsey / Rob & Em / Caf & Jenny / Edgar, Mirabelle, Ghislaine / Jonquil & Danny / Lizzie Fane / Jay & John / Ben Slater / Rich, Jonny, Phil / Georgie

Zena Alkayat
Kim Lightbody
Marente Van Der Valk
Alexander Breeze
Ben Brannan
Sarah Allberrey
Glenn Howard
Euan Ferguson
Sarah Chatwin
Hilary Bird
Rachel Ng

Anette xxx
Guy & Sam
Natasha & Daniel
Mum
Papa Chet & Kate
Marc, Ashley, Pyper, Lenny
Karen-o
Dumi, Rupa
Mahi, Prathiba
Yo, Mandy
Dantanarayana Clan
Batman & Catface